CW00321945

CANOEING

Skills and Techniques

CANOEING
Skills and Techniques

NEIL SHAVE

THE CROWOOD PRESS

First published in 1985 by
THE CROWOOD PRESS
Crowood House, Ramsbury
Marlborough, Wiltshire SN8 2HE

© Neil Shave 1985

Reprinted 1986
Paperback edition 1987
Paperback edition reprinted 1988, 1989, 1990

All rights reserved. No part of this publication may be reproduced or
transmitted in any form or by any means, electronic or mechanical,
including photocopy, recording, or any information storage and retrieval
system without permission in writing from the publishers.

Shave, Neil
    Canoeing: skills and techniques
    1. Canoes and canoeing
    I. Title
    797.1'22   GV783

    ISBN 0–946284–36–9 (HB)
        1–85223–026–6 (PB)

Acknowledgements

Neil Shave acknowledges the help of the following:
Calshot Activities Centre, Grenville College, National Scout Boating
Centre and Thames Young Mariners, for access to their facilities; the
many young canoeists who agreed to face the camera; Charles Willis,
photographer, for his assistance behind the camera; Alan Boatman, Bob
Gray, Nick Moore and Richard Ward for their support; and Jacqueline
Shapiro, for typing the manuscript.

Line illustrations by Annette Findlay

All photographs are taken by the author, except Fig 1 (Stuart Fisher), Figs
2, 19, 98 (Keith Williams), Figs 8, 43 (Malcolm Orvis), and Figs 31, 34, 93,
100 (Charles Willis).

Series Adviser C.E. Bond MEd, AdvDipPE, DLC (Hons), Head of PE,
Carnegie School of Physical Education and Human Movement Studies

Typeset by Inforum Ltd, Portsmouth
Printed and bound in Great Britain
by Redwood Press Ltd, Melksham

Contents

Neil Shave became a Senior Inland and Senior Sea Instructor in 1976. He has taught widely in the UK, West Germany, Holland, Belgium and France. In 1975 he founded the St Friendship Kayak Klub, a team of voluntary instructors specialising in assisting youth organisations with their canoeing activities.

Neil Shave has herein produced a concise but comprehensive guide to getting started in the popular pastime of canoeing.

Whether you seek thrills, excitement, or quiet enjoyment from your canoeing, this book provides sound advice, and numerous illustrations, on the equipment and techniques you will need to succeed in safety.

Neil's approach to explaining the skills required to control a canoe is a new one, and is an interesting and useful contribution to understanding basic techniques. The book is thoroughly recommended.

Geoff Good
Director of Coaching, British Canoe Union

My first taste of canoeing was on an Outward Bound course at the age of eighteen. My appet whetted, I wasted no time in learning all I could books and from the many friends who emerged from this new interest.

That was twelve years ago, and I can now loc back with happiness and pride at the hard work and achievements that made canoeing a way c for me. My principal interest has been in Wild W Racing, for which I am honoured to have been chosen to represent Britain at World Championships on several occasions.

Slalom and Marathon Racing have also featu but a few years ago I became interested in pass on the thrills and skills of the sport to youngster: The fact that I had paddled boats through some the roughest waters in the world did not mean t could automatically teach even the basics. To c so, it was necessary to qualify as a Senior Instructor, and it was on this course that I first m Neil Shave, as my Assessor! I quickly came to appreciate his depth of knowledge of basic canoeing techniques and how much more I had learn in order to instruct to his standard.

Although he has been teaching canoeing for many years, Neil has not wanted to work his wa the top and coach only the best in the land. Inst he has made a special study of basic skills and 1 easiest way for youngsters and their instructors master them.

I am delighted that he has at last put pen to paper, so that even more people can benefit fro the simplicity of his technique. Whilst it is true th the book has been written for beginners, I am certain that instructors will find its content of val and its approach refreshing. The explanations a very easy to follow, the photographs of young paddlers in action are very informative, and the layout and style is the clearest I have ever seen.

I hope that what you learn from this book will the foundation stone of your knowledge and he you towards experiencing as much enjoyment excitement as I have had from the wonderful wc of canoeing.

Sue Hornby

ntroduction

is possible to get into a canoe (or a *kayak* as ou will soon read) with no idea as to what to o, and paddle off. You will probably spend everal frustrating minutes going round in circes and then capsize. The boat is now updedown, you are in the water and in trouble. It may be that you have been in this situation efore and now want to learn properly, or you ay have learned a little already and now want to learn more. Either way, this book can help, as it contains all you need to know about equipment and technique to enable you to become a proficient canoeist and get the best out of this exciting and adventurous sport. You will be able to measure your progress by taking the graded tests of the British Canoe Union, and the following chapters cover all the canoeing skills up to the level of its Inland

g 1   Sue Hornby paddling her way to a Bronze Medal in the Wild Water
        Racing Team Event at the World Championships in Merano, Italy in
        1983. This was her third World Championship, having twice been a
        Gold Medallist in Commonwealth Championships, and three times the
        British Open Champion in the same discipline. Sue has also been
        National Sprint Champion and is currently a Premier Division Slalom
        paddler, a Wild Water Racing Competition Coach and a Senior Inland
        Instructor. She has the distinction of being the first woman to have
        canoed the famous Frazer Canyon in British Columbia, together with its
        notorious Hells Gate Rapid.

Introduction

Proficiency and Three Star Awards.

Age is no barrier. A youngster can learn to canoe just as soon as he is able to sit in the boat and hold the paddle, although it is not normally until he is about nine or ten years old that he will be able to take good control of a single-seater in moving water. Double-seaters and family size Canadian canoes, however, can include youngsters from a very early age.

It is not necessary to be able-bodied. Many of the less able are actively involved in the sport and amongst them are paddlers with widely differing and disabling conditions. Loss of use of the lower limbs simply means strapping them into the boat so that the arms can do the work, and less able arms may need the paddles strapped directly to them. Blindness is not a problem either, many of those so affected often paddling a double-seater with a normally sighted colleague as a partner.

Able-bodied or not, anybody taking up canoeing should remember that it is a physical activity and that some of the movements will need to be taken gently in the learning stage. Many simple home exercises will help considerably, particularly those involving trunk and shoulder rotation and their associated muscles.

As the intention of the book is not to be a specialised document for the less able or for fitness training, it has been written with the reasonably healthy young teenager in mind. Those not falling into this category may need to adapt the text to suit their personal circumstances, seeking medical advice or the recommendations of a department of the British Canoe Union as appropriate.

I do not believe that anybody can learn such a practical skill as canoeing only from a book; listening and watching and practising under a qualified instructor is the real answer. Use this book, therefore, for reference and background reading in conjunction with your water activity.

Happy paddling!

Origins

OW IT ALL BEGAN

arly three-quarters of the earth is covered
 sea, and much of the remaining land is
tted with lakes and criss-crossed by rivers.
om the earliest times, man has been forced
move about on this water, either in search
food, for trading or as part of his natural
sire to explore. Remote groups of people
t about building craft to suit their particular
eds, using whatever materials were avail-
le to them.

The results varied in length, width and con-
uction. The people who dwelt in the forests
d an abundant supply of logs and hollowed
m out to make boats. Later on, their boats
re made from planks of wood or from
oden frames covered with bark and water-
oofed with pitch. The people of the bare
tic wastes had only driftwood, but they had
 abundant supply of skins from the seals
d whales which they hunted for food and oil.
eir craft were of skins stretched over a
me of driftwood and bone.

It is from the development of these two
es of craft that the present-day canoes
ve come into being. The wooden ones from
 people of the forests developed in the
nds of the North American Indians. They
ed buffalo skins or birch-bark stretched
er wooden frames, to form an open boat in
ich one knelt and used a single-bladed
ddle. This style of boat has become known
 the Canadian Canoe and the practice of
eeling (or sitting back on one's heels) and
ng a single paddle is *canoeing*. The seal-
n over a driftwood or bone frame de-
oped in the hands of the Eskimos. Their

boats had covered-in decks with just a small
hole (cockpit) in which to sit, and their paddles
had a blade on each end. This form has
become known as the Eskimo Kayak and the
practice of sitting and using a double-bladed
paddle is *kayaking*. What you may have always called canoeing is probably, therefore,
really kayaking, but the word canoeing has
become the generic term for all aspects of the
sport in the British Isles.

The first sight of any such craft in the UK
was in 1865, when a Scottish barrister living in
London commissioned one to be made. His
name was John McGregor and his design
was based on what he had seen in North
America and on the east coast of Russia. It
was essentially a kayak, although it featured
a sail that could be used when the wind
was favourable. He called it *Rob Roy*. A year
later, in 1866, the first club was founded at
Twickenham (called simply The Canoe Club)
and, apart from becoming the Royal Canoe
Club seven years later at the command of
Queen Victoria, it remains active to this day.
The real canoe (usually referred to only as the
Canadian) was first seen in Europe in 1880.
Both forms of canoeing aroused great
interest (mainly touring) and in 1887 the British
Canoe Association was formed. Towards the
end of the century, however, canoeing activity
declined and it was not until the introduction
of folding boats in the early 1900s that interest
was rekindled.

In 1927, an Austrian called Pawlata read
some Eskimo papers and taught himself how
to perform the Eskimo Roll, a skill invented by
these arctic people as a means of righting
a canoe after capsize without getting out.

Origins

Pawlata's efforts were acknowledged by one of the rolls being named after him. In the early 1930s, an Englishman called Gino Watkins went to Greenland to explore the possibility of an air-route over the Arctic. His work involved close liaison with the Eskimos and he paddled with them and learned many of their kayaking techniques from first-hand experience. The cold waters of the Arctic meant that he had to learn to roll to survive.

The sport continued to develop and folding boats were made in London in 1933. Interest in competition was also evident, and canoeing made its first appearance in an Olympic Games in 1936 in Berlin, in the form of flat-water racing (now known as *sprint racing*). In the same year, the British Canoe Union was formed, the original Association of 1887 having faded out in the 1920s. Slalom racing (the art of negotiating a course on moving water) came to Britain in 1939, but with the outbreak of war, this and other organised events took an understandable back seat. The activities of Lt. Col. Hasler and his Cockleshell Heroes in Bordeaux Harbour, however, was evidence of the extent to which the skills of canoeing could be put to a very different use.

The post-war period proved to be one of intense activity and growth. In 1949, the first World Slalom Championships were held in Geneva, and Paul Farrant became the first British World Champion when he won a gold medal ten years later. In the early 1960s ca the first organised down-river racing (now w *water racing*) events and the trio of comp tive disciplines (sprint, slalom and wild wa racing) was complete. Over the years, the has had gold medalists in all these disciplin although the Eastern Block countries tend dominate in the only regular Olympic even sprint racing. Regular championships are h at all levels, the popular trio having been joir by the lesser known event of canoe saili Local competition exists within canoe surf and canoe polo circles, but this is not organised on an international level.

Not everybody, however, is paddl against the clock. Many – probably well o 250,000 – are happy to join friends and pa dle the waters of the rivers, the lakes and coastline for pleasure. Others travel furtl afield in order to explore the unknown particularly hazardous waters of the world great upsurge in expedition canoeing to place in the 1970s and British paddlers ha now successfully canoed along the Gra Canyon, down Mount Everest and arou Cape Horn.

The hope for the future is that more wa will become available for use by the public, enable the sport to continue to grow at levels, together with the excellent record safety that it already enjoys.

g 2 Richard Fox was World Slalom Champion in 1981 and retained the title in 1983, becoming the first person ever to do so. In addition, he is the only paddler to have been a member of the British team which won gold medals in three consecutive World Championships.

2 Equipment

THE BOAT

If you consider that there are both canoes and kayaks, for both competition and recreation, and for use inland and at sea, you will realise that the choice of craft is very wide. Amongst this variety are the kayaks designed for use on the moving water of a slalom course, the earlier versions of which can also be used with great success on most other types of water. The skills required to paddle it are a good foundation and are easily adapted to the more specialised skills required in other craft. These factors have resulted in this boat being the one chosen for most general situations. The book concentrates on the skills relating to it, restricting mention of the many other types and their uses to the last chapter.

Construction (Fig 3)

The shapes of these general slalom boats can vary, although they all have a similar length and width.

They are light, hard-wearing and made from plastic or glass reinforced plastic. Boats of this latter material (usually referred to as *fibreglass*) can be made in moulds by do-it-yourself enthusiasts. One of the newer synthetic materials (Kevlar and Diolen) may be built into them to strengthen the construction. Canvas is now seldom used on account of the ease with which it damages, although wood is still used, particularly for kits.

A knowledge of the general features of a kayak is essential and these should always be checked carefully for damage before going afloat.

Bow and Stern

These are respectively the front and bac[k] being usually pointed and therefore subject [to] damage in inexperienced hands. Check f[or] cracks or holes.

Gunwale Line

This is the edge of the boat, being the seam [of] fibre-glass boats where the two halves hav[e] been made in separate moulds and joine[d] together. It is a common place for leaks, eith[er] from poor construction or as a result [of] youngsters playing bumper cars! You ca[n] check for splits by placing the boat on its sid[e] and pressing above and below the seam.

Hull

The bottom half of the boat and therefore th[e] part most likely to develop leaks after ground[l]ing or rock-bashing. Check by careful inspe[c]tion. The top half is called the deck and is les[s] liable to damage.

Fig 3 (opposite) Different designs of slalom boat. Lisa (right) is holding the older design, which is bulky and difficult to manoeuvre, but good for touring. Nic is holding a more modern design, which has increased rocker to facilitate turning and dipping the ends under slalom poles. Charlotte is holding a very modern design, where the ends have been tapered to points and the overall volume has been reduced to the minimum necessary to support the weight of the paddler. This latter design is ideal for competition use, but can easily cause damage and be damaged in general situations.

Toggles *(Figs 4 & 5)*

These should be fitted to both ends of boats in general use. A toggle is the safest way of keeping hold of a boat if you end up out of it and in the water, although many new craft are supplied without them. A popular alternative is just a loop of rope, an end-loop.

End-loops are easier and cheaper to fit, but using them requires putting your fingers through the loop. This is particularly danger-ous in moving water, because if you have fallen out of your boat and are holding on to it by the end-loop, your hand can be seriously injured. This can occur if the boat is turned over a few times by the turbulence of the water, causing the loop to twist and tighten on

Fig 4   Toggle and end-loop. The end-loop is frequently found on competition boats, as it is less likely to hit a pole during slalom work. The toggle is safer and more comfortable to use, by holding with two fingers on either side of its rope.

Fig 5   End-loop danger. This tightening effect (called tourniquet effect) is very dangerous and, if not released quickly, can inflict permanent damage.

your fingers. It is extremely painful and can be very difficult to release.

Cockpit

This is where you sit and is more or less in the middle of the boat. Newcomers to canoeing often have difficulty in telling which end of the craft is which, but can do so by looking care-fully at the cockpit and seat. The front of the cockpit is usually more pointed than the back and the seat is usually set slightly towards the back of the cockpit opening. The narrow lip around the edge of the cockpit is called the *coaming* and holds the spraydeck in place. Always check that the seat is not loose, that the coaming is not coming away from the deck and that there are no sharp edges.

ɔotrest *(Fig 6)*

ese come in a variety of forms, the most
ɔular being a bar of metal bolted from one
e of the hull to the other, two pedal-like
ts (one on each side), or a bulkhead (wall)
ɔss the entire inside of the boat. A footrest
s two important uses other than simply
ɔewhere to rest your feet:

It is a vital contact point, transmitting the
ddling power that has come through your
ns, shoulders, back, bottom, legs and feet,
the boat.
In any situation where the canoe stops
ddenly, it is the only thing that will stop you
ding down inside the boat. This would be a

most dangerous situation if you were then to
capsize, as it would be extremely difficult to
get out. The action of stopping suddenly
would need to be fairly forceful, perhaps by
hitting a rock head-on.

A footrest should have each of two important
features:

1. It should be adjustable. Its distance from
the seat will need to be changed not only as
you grow, but also according to whether you
are wearing light summer clothes and plim-
solls, or several winter layers and thicker soled
footwear.
2. It must *fail-safe*. This only applies to the bar
type, and is vital if a sudden stopping action

ɾ 6 *Fail-safe footrest. The bar is held on flanges on either side of the inside of
the boat. It can swing forwards out of its plastic clip on the left, pivoting
on the wing nut. Note the block buoyancy at the front of the boat, having
been secured so firmly in place that it adds strength to the deck and the
hull.*

Equipment

forces your feet over or under it. As you pull your feet towards you again, the footrest must collapse. This is achieved by one end being hinged so that the other can swing towards you.

Buoyancy *(Fig 7)*

Most canoe building materials do not float. If you find this strange, consider that many ships are made from metal! The kayak (like any other boat) only floats when its weight is not greater than the weight of the water it displaces. If your boat weighs 15kg and you weigh 40kg, you will displace 55 kg of water. As soon as you and the boat are heavier than

the water you displace, the boat sinks. This easy to demonstrate by filling it up complete with water.

It is important that the canoe floats ev when full of water, not only so that it is not lc after a capsize, but so that it floats enough give you a sort of life-raft for extra support the water. To achieve this, the boat should packed with a very buoyant material, to stop ever filling up completely with water. The mc suitable material is block polystyrene, pack securely and evenly into both ends, so that t boat still floats level when flooded.

Fig 7   Block buoyancy. This should extend the entire length of the back of the boat, from immediately behind the seat. It also strengthens the deck and the hull, particularly if you sit on the back deck when getting in or out. Note that there is a block at the side of the seat, thus preventing it moving when under strain. The slot in the seat is for a backstrap.

Fig 8   (opposite) Using a spraydeck. Nick's descent of Rhayader Falls on the River Wye sinks his boat almost entirely and would be foolhardy if the boat were to fill up with water. The modern spraydeck prevents this and is strong enough to withstand the pressure of gallons of water on it.

OTHER EQUIPMENT

Spraydeck *(Figs 8 & 9)*

This is a garment worn around the waist and designed so that it fits over the edge of the cockpit. It prevents water getting into the boat.

The modern spraydeck is a long way from the original Eskimo ones of sealskin and thong. It can be made from nylon, a waterproof backed fabric or neoprene rubber and is released by giving a sharp pull on a release strap, fixed either to the front or to either side.

Always check that your release strap is visible and firmly attached. If you ever find yourself upsidedown and the release strap is hidden or has broken, it is an easy matter to pull the spraydeck elastic away from the cockpit coaming and release it.

A spraydeck should never be worn until you have practised releasing it in a supervised training situation. Nylon and fabric spraydecks may have an adjustable waist elastic or a shoulder strap. Both are useful additions.

Buoyancy Aids and Life-jackets *(Figs 10 & 11)*

One or the other is essential for all canoeing, but there is a clear difference between the two. The buoyancy aid is simply an aid to buoyancy. It is a sort of padded waistcoat, fitted with an adjustable waist-band and

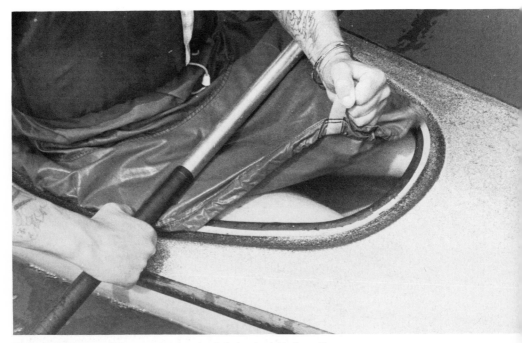

Fig 9   Release strap. If it is necessary to get out of a boat quickly, it must be
possible to remove the spraydeck immediately. A sharp tug on the
release strap and the elastic springs away from the cockpit lip.

ometimes with a thick collar. It does not flate.

If you are in the water, it will keep you afloat nd leave you free to use your energies to eep hold of the boat, look where you are oing or wave to attract attention. For maxi- um efficiency it must be a good fit and be orn correctly, by ensuring that the waist- and is tied securely so that it grips under your os. If not, it may float up over your face.

The life-jacket acts as a buoyancy aid when orn normally, but it can be inflated. This will ot only increase its buoyancy, but also turn ou over onto your back and keep your face ut of the water. It must never be inflated uring normal activity, but only when you are the water and in need of its life-saving roperties.

For general canoeing purposes, the buoy- ancy aid is sufficient. It is less expensive, and easier and more comfortable to wear. How- ever, some clubs may insist on a life-jacket and the advice of your activity leader should be followed.

Whichever you wear, make sure that it is of an approved type. Approval is always marked and should be by BCU (British Canoe Union) or SBBNF (Ship and Boat Builders National Federation) for buoyancy aids, or by BSI (Brit- ish Standards Institute) for life-jackets.

Paddles *(Fig 12)*

These are your means of power and come in different shapes and sizes. The whole thing is

ç 10 *Incorrectly worn buoyancy aid. This looks amusing, but is a dangerous and frightening situation if it happens during an emergency. This youngster cannot breathe properly or see anything, and his movement is restricted. It is easily prevented by tying the waist band firmly so that it grips under the ribs.*

Fig 11 Inflated life-jacket. A life-jacket should only ever be inflated in the water,
either because you may be there for a long time or because you are
frightened by the situation. Ricky is wearing it properly and it keeps him
floating comfortably on his back with his face well clear of the water.

'g 12   Feathered paddles. As Nicholas paddles away, you can see that whilst
the blade in the water is working, the blade in the air is at 90° to it and
cutting through the air. Note that this blade is curved.

Equipment

called a paddle (or a pair of paddles), the flattened pieces on each end being the *blades* and the long pole-like structure in the middle being the *shaft*.

Each blade is set into the shaft at right angles to the other. This is called *feathering* and its main purpose is to reduce the resistance of the air on the blade not in the water. If this were not so, one blade would always be pushing air, an action that would require additional effort.

Paddle Construction

The different materials used in manufacture affect performance, weight and cost.

Wood was the material used by primitive man, although it is now the most expensive. The correct manufacture of wooden paddles is a highly skilled occupation and is achieved by glueing together many layers of different woods with varying degrees of hardness. The process is called *laminating* and laminated paddles may be all wood, or laminated blades in an alloy or glass-fibre shaft. A paddle carved from a single piece of wood lacks strength and elasticity.

Plywood is a less expensive alternative to wood, but is only used for blades. It is normally marine-ply, which is prepared and treated to withstand prolonged immersion in water.

Aluminium and its alloys, especially those developed in the aircraft industry, are used for the shaft and sometimes as a strengthener in plastic blades. The shafts are both light and strong, but often cold to hold. Many now have a plastic covering.

Fibre-glass may be the material for boats, but it is one of the least common for paddles. For blades it tends to bend and be liable to split, although in tubular form, it makes a light and very strong shaft.

Plastic has become popular and is good value for money. There are a number of compounds under this general heading, all of which are strong, resilient and used principally in the manufacture of blades.

Shaft Design (Figs 13 & 14)

The shaft's length governs the overall length of the paddle. This is ideal when, with the paddle standing upright on the ground, your fingers can curl over the top blade.

A slightly shorter paddle may be preferred for the advanced strokes of moving water work and a slightly longer paddle may suit a touring or racing situation. All shafts have a similar diameter, although a shaft may not be circular for its entire length. It may be oval where the hands grip, each oval being at right angles to the other. This is an advantage as it greatly assists in maintaining a correct grip. If this has not been done during manufacture, alloy shafts can be re-shaped by squeezing them slightly in a vice.

Blade Design (Figs 15 & 16)

The surface areas of blades are fairly constant, but the exact outlines may differ:

1. Metal tipped blades reduce the damaging effect of hitting rocks in a boulder strewn or shallow rapid.
2. A curve along the length of the blade gives it a better bite in the water (*Fig 12*).
3. A rib or ridge along the length of the blade helps stop it quivering when under power.
4. Asymmetric blades are not square at their ends, resulting in them entering the water more evenly and providing more power at the start of the stroke. They are usually restricted to racing paddles.

Fig 13   Ideal paddle length. This simple test before you go afloat will ensure
that you have a paddle of a length that matches your size and reach.

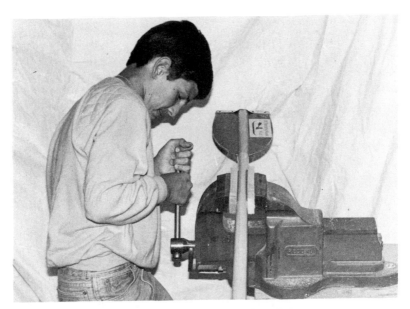

Fig 14   Shaft ovalling. This can only be applied to aluminium shafts and must
be done carefully. Use a felt pen to mark your normal hand position on
the shaft, and squeeze that part gently in a vice. The shaft should be
protected from the jaws of the vice with pieces of wood and the oval
should be just enough to be felt. Too much will weaken the shaft and
make it liable to bend. Only the control side need be done, and for the
ovalling to be at the correct angle, the blade must be horizontal as
shown.

Choice of Paddle

The most important thing is to have the paddle
the correct length, thereafter you get what you
pay for. It is not, however, worth paying a lot
for a paddle when you are young. Much as
you can normally shorten a paddle that is too
long, it is almost impossible to lengthen a
paddle as you grow. The ideal ones are probably those sold in kit form, where the shaft can
be sawn to your length before assembly, and
the blades only need a few coats of good
varnish before being screwed or glued into
each end. Flat bladed paddles can be used
right or left-handed, but curved blades cannot. They are set to the shaft for use either one
way or the other. To check that you have the
correct ones, when the front of the blade is
facing you in your control hand (the normal
paddle grip), the non-control blade should
have its front facing up in the air.

Crash Helmets

This may give the impression that canoeing is
highly dangerous, but it is not so. There are
however, situations when you might get an
accidental bang on the head from a friend's
paddle or capsize and hit your head on a rock.
For general canoeing a lightweight and relatively inexpensive crash helmet is available. It
is made of fibre-glass or hard plastic, has lots
of holes (to let the water out) and no foam
padding (which would absorb water and become very heavy). The head is supported
within the helmet by an adjustable plastic
cradle. Many of the different designs can be
seen in the photographs throughout the book.

Repair Kit

There is a variety of items that you will find
essential, being either bits for repairing the
boat or bits for repairing yourself. It is advis-
able to build up your own kit and make sure

g 15   Metal tipped blades. Both these blades have been subjected to the
same use, but the protection afforded by the metal tip on one is
obvious. The damage is only caused by the normal wear and tear of
learners hitting the bottom, bank or boat from time to time.

ɔu have it with you on all canoeing projects.

ooking after Yourself

his kit could be just a few pieces of plaster for
ɪat unwelcome blister or cut, but should
ɪclude any other item that you are capable of
sing. Almost any accident can happen dur-
g a canoeing activity, including the major
roblems of breaking a leg by slipping on wet
ɔcks, or cutting yourself wide open by hitt-
g your head on them. These conditions
ɔviously require immediate action, particu-
rly where bleeding (internal or external) is
ɔncerned. If possible, prepare yourself to be
ɔle to deal with such problems by attending
first aid course.

Life-saving skills are also very important,
though they require no special equipment.
ɔu owe it to your friends afloat to be able to
wim them to safety if necessary, as well as
ɔply artificial respiration in an emergency. It is
a good idea to join a school or local life-saving
club and study for the appropriate awards.

If you are travelling away from a base, you
should also consider spare clothing (minimum
of jumper, trousers and towel), high energy
food (chocolate or dates), a full thermos flask,
a whistle (for attracting attention) and a torch.

Waterproof Containers (Fig 17)

The larger plastic food containers are ideal,
but many of the containers used in industry
and in the Armed Forces have been adopted
by canoeists as standard equipment. There
are also specially manufactured canoeists'
containers, in the form of long plastic bags.
These are ideal for clothing and pack well on
either side of any block buoyancy. All containers must be secured in place and must never
be carried between or around the legs, as they
could prevent you getting out after a capsize.

Fig 16 Asymmetric blades. Both blades are being held at about the angle that they will enter the water during normal forward paddling. It is clear that the asymmetric blade (left) will enter its entire width almost at once, whilst the conventional shape will start with only a corner. This can be critical in racing situations, for which the quicker and more even bite of the asymmetric blade is normally chosen.

Towing-line

This will enable you to help a tired or injured colleague by towing him to safety. The line is specially made, with a clip on one end for fixing it to your patient's boat, normally the toggle. You may tow by having a non-slip loop diagonally across your chest and over one shoulder, although it is more common for the rope to be fixed to a special clip just behind the cockpit. The important thing is for you to be able to release it from yourself or your boat quickly in the event of capsize or other problem. In order to avoid the snatch of the rope as the slack is taken up by the towing action, a piece of thick elastic (shock cord) is normally built into the line.

Fig 17 Boat repair. A lot can be done with PVC tape and a pair of scissors, providing the repair area has been thoroughly dried. Note the screw top waterproof plastic containers that are ideal for repair and first aid kits, spare clothing and food. The contents of the larger container have been further protected by a plastic bag.

Deck-lines

These are found on boats used for touring, being rope (normally 6mm diameter) that runs around the edge of the deck. Its principal use is as a grab-line, making it easier for anybody in the water to hold on to your boat. It may also be used for tying a boat to a mooring. The most important thing is for any line to be tight. A slack rope (especially near the cockpit) could catch your hand whilst paddling, or your neck if you were in the water.

CLOTHING

This depends so much on the time of year and what you are doing, that hard and fast rules are difficult to set. You may be training for half an hour in an indoor swimming pool or you may be off with a few friends for an October weekend of river canoe-camping. The following notes should be borne in mind when deciding the exact requirements of a particular situation.

Swimwear

This is ideal in the summer months and if you are very likely to capsize. It is not, however, very warm and is often not comfortable to wear when seated for long periods. In colder months, therefore, you may choose to wear everyday underwear.

Body

It is not so much the air temperature that dictates how warm you are, but rather the wind and how wet you are. Even a light summer wind will have a noticeable chilling effect on a wet body. Always wear or carry a windproof top, ideally of a single layer nylon, so that it can double as a waterproof. These are readily available in High Street stores as anoraks or cagoules, although special canoeing ones are sold by appropriate boating shops.

On a very hot summer's day a T-shirt may be fine, but your choice of clothing should be towards materials (notably wool) that trap a layer of air next to the skin. If you wear a woollen jumper and a cagoule you will probably be warmer (and more comfortable) than a friend wearing a vest, a T-shirt, a sports shirt, a nylon sweater and a windcheater.

Legs

The legs are normally protected from the wind by being in the boat, more so if you have advanced to wearing a spraydeck. Water can be more of a problem, as it drips off your hands during paddling and lands in your lap. Shorts are normally sufficient in the summer months, but remember that you will be exposed to the full force of any wind or weather when you get out. Long trousers, particularly track suit trousers, are definitely warmer, but very heavy and uncomfortable when wet. Nylon overtrousers on top of shorts is a good compromise, or on top of warm long trousers during the colder months.

Wet-suits *(Fig 18)*

These are the neoprene rubber suits worn by most skin-divers, in which a layer of water is trapped between the rubber and the skin and heated by the body. Full wet-suits have no real place in canoeing, due to the restriction experienced by the sleeves. A combined neoprene vest and long trousers (long-john) or short trousers (shortie), however, can be very useful, especially in the colder months of the year or when the risk of capsize is high. Only swimwear and possibly a T-shirt need be worn underneath, although a cagoule is normally necessary, as neoprene is not totally windproof.

Footwear

Always wear something. Not only is it more comfortable (particularly when carrying your boat), but river banks and beaches are notorious for broken glass. If you are unfortunate enough to capsize, you may have to touch the river bed, an even more popular rubbish dump. Never wear wellingtons, as they are extremely heavy when full of water and make swimming almost impossible. Old trainers are a good choice, but beware of the style where the tread goes up over the toe and back up the heel. Incidents have arisen when the tread of the toe and heel has become jammed between the deck and hull of the boat. Neoprene footwear (known as booties) is ideal but expensive.

Head and Hands

A third of your body heat can escape through your scalp. On a hot day that may help to keep you cool, but at other times it can lead to rapid cooling and its associated hazards. A woollen bobble hat is ideal and will also give you quite a lot of protection from the rain.

Gloves are not recommended, as your grip on the paddle will be hindered. There are special canoeing gloves available (called poggies), but these should not be necessary for general canoeing use. The long sleeves of jumper to keep your wrists warm and a ligh grip on the paddle to allow blood to circulat into your fingers will go a long way toward ensuring warm hands.

Fig 18　Canoeing clothing. Vivian is putting on a perfect cold weather combination. He is already wearing a neoprene long-john over a thermal T-shirt, and is pulling on a canoeing cagoule. Note the rubber cuff on his wrist that will stop water going up his arm, and the velcro and neoprene rubber collar that can be fastened for a similar effect.

3 Safety

well-known canoeist once said, 'If you don't ant to drown, don't go near water'. None of ; wants to drown, but many of us want to be ear, on or in the water. We must, therefore, ke a risk that is balanced between being vare of the various dangers and taking all the ecessary precautions.

Everything you do is concerned with safety. hether you are selecting the boat, the cloth- g or the stroke you will use, every aspect of our equipment and technique contributes wards a safer enjoyment of the sport.

The whole book, therefore, is about safety, ut this chapter mentions those special fac- rs that are neither equipment nor technique, d ignorance of which could lead to a serious d possibly life-threatening condition. The formation is as important for every water oortsman as it is for you as a canoeist.

BILITY TO SWIM

his may sound obvious, but the fact that you ay be able to swim length after length of the cal swimming pool, does not necessarily ake you a good swimmer from a canoeing oint of view. Not only does a swim during anoeing often start from a position of being osidedown in a boat in cold, moving and ometimes dirty water, but you will be clothed d wearing a buoyancy aid.

Every canoeist must be able to swim fifty etres in the clothing and in the water on hich he will be working. Do not assume that ou can do it, but arrange for a properly upervised opportunity to try it. You will be mazed how much the cold water will sap

your energy and how much your clothing will change your natural buoyancy and drag you to a standstill.

EXPOSURE

This has the medical name of hypothermia, and is a condition that can be a serious risk in any outdoor activity, particularly where water is involved. It is caused by a reduction of the body temperature from its normal level of about 37°C. You may well have heard a news bulletin about a search for climbers or sailors being abandoned after a few days as 'there can be no further hope of survival'. It will have been calculated that the cold of the mountains or the water will have killed the casualties, let alone the effect of any other injury. The prob- lem with water is that it causes the body to lose heat twenty-seven times faster than when it is dry. Movement of the arms and legs aggravates the situation as it causes the heart to beat faster and supply more blood to the muscles for energy. These muscles will already be cold and will cool the blood even more.

Prevention is much better than cure. You must understand that the T-shirt and shorts you wear when you set off on a canoeing trip in the brilliant sunshine, are inadequate when the sky clouds over, and dangerous when it rains or you fall in. *Always* have some spare clothes and windproofs handy on the bank or beach if you are staying in one area, or with you in the boat if you are travelling around.

The onset of exposure is very slow and is often not noticed by the sufferer. You will,

Fig 19   Safety and skill. Coping with this sort of water safely requires a high
          degree of skill and experience. Jane Roderick can smile as she does
          so, having proven her ability by winning a silver medal in the World
          Slalom Championships in 1983.

vever, notice it in a friend, who will not only
very cold, but often start to behave dif-
ntly. Slurred speech, not hearing properly,
ring requests, or complaining of blurred
on are some of the signs. The situation is
gerous and you must stop, wrap the
ualty up in everything dry and warm you
find and summon medical help. A plastic
vival bag or space blanket is by far the best
of retaining body heat and should be
uded in your day trip kit.

EATHER

n and sun will each have their own ways of
cting your enjoyment of an activity, but
h will also have an effect on its safety.
derstanding the weather is an interesting
ject, but predicting it is difficult – even for
professionals. There are many books on
subject, but the following general notes
line points of importance for the canoeist.

w Pressure

v pressure areas (cyclones) are usually
racterised by strong winds and rain, a
fect combination of conditions for expo-
e. Remember to take all the necessary
cautions. Rain will also cause river water
els to rise and change a placid stream into a
ng torrent. You may get swept into over-
nging branches or you may encounter trees
t have been uprooted and swept down-
am.

gh Pressure

h pressure areas (anti-cyclones) are usual-
haracterised by clear skies and good visi-
y. It is generally good canoeing weather,
ough the temperature can be quite cold
side of the summer season. You may need

to protect yourself against the effects of the
sun, which not only shines down on you, but is
reflected up at you by your boat and the water.
There are two dangers, sunburn and sunstroke. Sunburn may be familiar to you, but do
not underestimate how fast it can affect you
when you are on the water. Cover yourself
with suitable clothing or apply an appropriate
cream. Do not forget to protect underneath
your arms, chin and nose as these areas are
first affected by the reflection from the water.
Sunstroke is an unpleasant and sometimes
dangerous condition, characterised by giddi-
ness and sickness. To prevent it, avoid sunburn and keep the sun off your head and neck,
possibly by wearing a neckerchief or brimmed
hat. Always have plenty of drinks available.

Wind

Winds coming from the north or east are
normally cold but dry, winds coming from the
west and south are normally moist but warm.

Wind speeds are greater over open water,
where there are no houses, trees or other
obstacles to slow it down. A river valley can
often act like a funnel, attracting the wind to
blow along it and speeding it up as it does so.

On lakes or the sea, an on-shore wind
means that you are likely to be blown ashore if
you have to stop paddling for any reason. An
off-shore wind blows you away from the safety of the shore.

GROUP

Never canoe alone. For all that you might be a
good swimmer and may never have capsized
previously, mistakes are made by even the
best and most experienced paddlers. A freak
wave, a momentary lapse in concentration or
a submerged post can cause a quick capsize
and it is a very skilled person who can then get

Safety

back into his boat unaided. This becomes impossible if the boat is waterlogged or if you are tired or injured. A dislocated shoulder or violent stomach ache may make it impossible for you to paddle to safety and you cannot tow yourself!

The motto is 'less than three there sho never be'. It takes two canoeists to rescu capsized paddler safely, and in serious cas one can stay with the casualty while the ot goes for help.

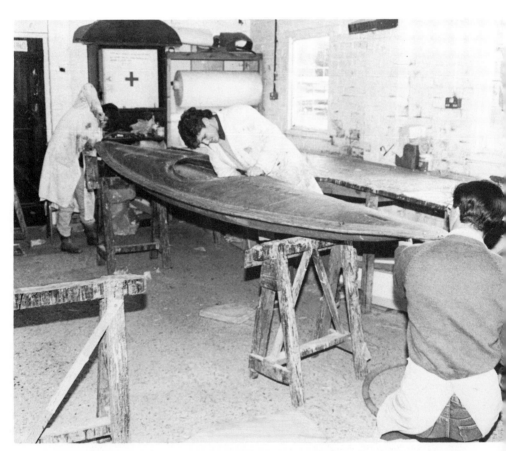

Fig 20   Safety and equipment. The best equipment is born of good workshop practice. This boat is being made on a course at the National Scout Boating Centre. Note the clean working area, the protective clothing and the first aid kit.

4 Going Afloat

CARRYING THE BOAT
(Fig 21)

Much as you may find it easier to carry one or two boats between two of you, you should work towards being able to handle a boat yourself. The shoulder carry is then the most comfortable.

When lifting a boat, avoid straining yourself by getting it from the ground to waist level by bending your knees, *not* your back. Never drag a boat to the waterside. On all but the thickest grass, the ground has a similar effect to sandpaper.

LAUNCHING THE BOAT
(Figs 22 & 23)

The water's edge is likely to present one of three general situations:

1. A beach. Simply put the boat on the water so that it is just afloat.

Fig 21   Carrying the boat. When you can manage this shoulder carry, you can get on and off the water without help. Take care to get the boat properly balanced. Note that Charlie's right hand is steering and steadying by holding the front of the cockpit.

Fig 22 Launching the boat. Justine is using the knee-nudging technique to launch without hitting the edge of the jetty. Note that the paddle is within easy reach.

2. A steep bank or jetty with a drop of up to about 50cm. Place the boat on the edge of the bank, and lift it from the non-water side by holding under the edge of the cockpit nearest you. Rest the kayak on your thighs, and with a quick leg bending action, nudge it away, keeping hold whilst it drops onto the water. Make sure the paddle is close enough to reach without letting go of the boat.

3. A drop of over about 50cm. Slide your boat in end first, keeping the paddle in one hand. When you are forced to let go of the boat, maintain control of it by poking one end of the paddle into the cockpit.

GETTING IN

This can be a little unstable, as your centre of gravity is too high until you are seated. It is important therefore, to keep your contact with the boat (and therefore your weight) over its centre.

The techniques described are for beginners, and you will be able to combine some of the moves into a single action or develop other methods as your experience grows. Make sure that the paddle is alongside where you are getting in, so that you can reach it from the boat.

From a Beach (Fig 24)

Place the boat afloat so that when you are standing in it, it only just touches the bottom. Get in and sit down. A push with the paddle upright on one side and a hand on the ground on the other and you are afloat.

23 Distant boat control. When launching from a high bank, there is a point
when you are forced to let go of the boat. Have the paddle handy to
hold the boat alongside while you clamber down the bank and get in.

Fig 24   Beach launch. Although the boat starts off afloat, getting in often
makes it go aground. Ease it free by pushing down with the paddle on
one side and a hand on the other.

25 Getting in from a bank. Your weight must be kept over the centre of the boat and your arms braced to stop the boat drifting away. Ricky's hand and foot are perfectly central so that he can take his weight off the jetty without the boat tipping over. Note that the paddle is close by.

rom a Low Bank or Jetty
igs 25 & 26)

With the boat on the water alongside, sit the bank facing the front.

Grip the centre of the back of the cockpit th the hand nearest the boat, your fingers side.

Place the other hand on the ground im-ediately behind your bottom.

Place the foot nearest the boat into the iddle of the cockpit, just in front of the seat.

You should now be able to lift your bottom f the ground, your weight being spread cross both hands and both feet. You can op the boat floating away, by pulling your ms and legs towards each other.

Place your other foot in the boat and swing ur bottom over the seat. As you lower your-self onto the seat, straighten your legs into the front of the boat.

7. If the water is flowing fast and wants to sweep the boat away as you are getting in, or if your arms and shoulders are not strong enough to hold the boat alongside as de-scribed, it may be necessary to make use of the paddle. Lay it carefully across the back of the cockpit and onto the jetty or shore. Put your hands (and therefore weight) over the points where the paddle touches the back of the cockpit and the bank, and the boat will remain stable alongside. Failure to keep your weight over these points of contact may result in bending or damaging the shaft or blades.

From a High Bank or Jetty

The exact technique will depend on the height

Fig 26   Getting in with paddle support. This is not recommended for regular
use, but may be necessary if you are not strong enough to hold the
boat firmly alongside. Elaine has the boat securely fixed, by bracing it
under the paddle and her weight. Apart from the disadvantage of
possible damage to the paddle, this method involves having the
paddle behind you, when you will need it in front of you to paddle off.

of the drop, but the general principle of keeping your weight over the centre is critical. You will probably need to lower yourself down to the boat and then stand in front of the seat with both feet. Sit down (with your knees up) to recover your balance, then lift your weight with one hand on either side of the cockpit and straighten your legs.

From Knee-deep Water
(Fig 27)

1. Stand alongside the boat facing forward and with your paddle in the hand nearest the boat.
2. Hold on to the far side of the cockpit with this hand and place the foot nearest the boat inside it, but with no weight on it.

3. Straighten the leg into the boat, at the same time holding the side of the cockpit nearest you with your other hand behind you.
4. Simultaneously drop your bottom onto the seat and lift the weight off your standing leg, leaving it hanging over the side.
5. Steady yourself with your hands still one on each side of the cockpit, lift your weight off the seat, bring the other leg into the boat, straighten it and sit down again as quickly as you can.

CORRECT SEATING POSITION

To paddle properly, your boat needs to be good a fit on you as shoes need to be if you are to run properly.

Fig 27   Getting in from the water. Charlie is at the point where he is
straightening his right leg into the boat and dropping his bottom onto
the seat. This forces him to lift the leg in the water and take his weight
on his hands. They are spaced evenly on either side of the boat, one
holding the paddle.

The Seat

Most youngsters use full size kayaks, meaning that the seat is often too wide. A lot of the power of paddling is transmitted to the boat through your bottom, so it should be snug in its seat.

In addition, if you are not in the middle of the seat, your weight distribution will be uneven and the boat will tend to turn. The problem is easy to solve by strapping some waterproof padding to the inside of the sides of the seat. Make it a snug fit, but not so tight that it jams you in.

Legs

Sit with your knees jammed upwards underneath the deck and outwards towards the sides of the canoe. It is gripping with your knees that helps you to sit upright, helps you to maintain your balance and helps to transmit the effect of any turning stroke to the boat. If you find that the muscles on the inside of your thighs ache after a spell of paddling, you are doing it properly. It will happen less as you become fitter!

Feet

They should be firmly against the footrest, with your heels on the bottom (hull) of the boat. More about your feet is explained in the section on footrests.

Body

With your bottom, knees and feet firmly in place, you should be able to bend forwards, backwards, sideways or twist without losing

Going Afloat

your grip. Most paddling is undertaken sitting upright, if not leaning slightly forward, but you will need all the other movements in other strokes. Never submit to laziness and lean against the back of the cockpit. You will no have the same control and might possibly los your balance.

Fig 28   Oops! This is not Alan getting into trouble, but getting out of it. He is on the rapids at Symonds Yat (River Wye), and has accidentally leant upstream. This inevitably led to a capsize, from which he is now recovering by rolling up on the downstream side. The photograph shows a perfect hip-flick, with the boat on its way up and the body following. These terms should become clear as you study the following chapters.

Coming Ashore

is involves getting out of the boat and lifting out of the water. The skills are almost the verse of getting in, with the added problems getting out when the boat is upsidedown d emptying it before you get back in.

ETTING OUT *(Fig 29)*

e main problem with reversing the getting in procedure is that you have to lift your body, rather than lower it. It is even more difficult when a bank or jetty is involved. The action can be simplified as follows:

1. Put the paddle on the bank or jetty.
2. If your legs are short enough to enable you to bend them and bring your feet up to the seat, do so. If not, put one hand on either side of the cockpit and lift yourself enough to bend

29 Getting out. You will find this method ideal if you can get your knees up in the cockpit. The boat is partly braced by the paddle as Ricky gets onto his feet, by pulling with one hand on the cockpit and pushing with the other on the side. He is keeping his weight low and over the centre of the boat until he is able to step out.

your knees and bring your feet up. If there is not enough room to sit on the seat again, sit on the back of the cockpit or boat (depending on its strength).

3. From either of these positions stand up. The easier way is to hold on to the front of the cockpit with the hand furthest from the bank and pull as you stand. The other hand is on the bank or jetty keeping the boat alongside.

4. Only in difficult situations should it be necessary to brace the boat to the shore with the paddle behind you.

CAPSIZE DRILL

This is the procedure for getting out of the boat when it is upsidedown. It should be

practised again and again, in preparation the day when you capsize by accident a your actions need to be reflex. The best way start is in a swimming pool, with a compete person standing alongside. Then move on normal canoeing water with other paddle around and ready to help. It is very difficult get stuck in the boat, but fairly easy to fright or bruise yourself. Careful practice will avc either.

The Basic Drill *(Figs 30 to 32*

1. Sit correctly, with special attention to gr ping with your knees and leaning forward. F your arms round the front of the boat (l hugging) and capsize.

2. When upsidedown, both your hands

Fig 30   Capsize drill. Being upsidedown in a swimming pool, you have the comfort of warm and clear water in which to practise. Note that Nick is able to watch through the water to see that all is going well.

31 *Getting out upsidedown. Watching Spud underwater, you can see the pronounced forward roll as he keeps his head forward and pushes with his hands on the edge of the cockpit. The action is just like taking off a pair of trousers.*

out of the water (one on each side). Bang e bottom of the boat three times with both, owly and firmly. This is a practice routine to elp build your confidence in being upside-own as well as to make you maintain the grip ith your knees and not try to get out of the oat before it is properly upsidedown.

Bring your hands back underwater and lease the spraydeck (if worn).

Place one hand on each side of the cockpit oaming, just in front of you and push down lbeit really up) with both hands, releasing the ip with your knees and leaning forward at e same time. This is a most important move-ent and is very similar to taking off a pair of ousers.

You should forward somersault out of the oat and surface at the side. After your first apsize you will probably have no idea which ay round you are (disorientation).

Keep hold of the boat, *leave it upside-*

down, but do not try to climb onto it.

7. Swim to one end (the front if possible), keeping in contact with the boat all the time and leaving it upsidedown.

8. Once at the end, lay on your back, hold the end of the boat over one shoulder and kick your legs (breast-stroke or life-saving kick fashion) to safety. You will be able to hold the boat with one hand, leaving the other free to hold the paddle or help swim.

There are two very important aspects to the routine.

Firstly, always get out with a forward somer-sault. There is a natural tendency to relax your legs and body as you capsize, allowing you to lean back and twist in the cockpit as you go over. Do not. This action not only causes you to bruise your thighs on the cockpit edge, but can create the one situation where a leg (from the knee to the heel) can become jammed

37

Fig 32 *Swimming with the boat. The perfect position is with the bow on the shoulder and the buoyancy of the boat being used as a support by hanging underneath. This and the action of the buoyancy aid will keep your head well clear of the water. Note that the paddle is being held firmly while the legs kick to safety.*

across the width of the boat.

Secondly, leave the kayak upsidedown. The boat contains a considerable amount of air and is therefore very buoyant. It can act as a life-raft if you need some extra support, not by climbing onto it but by hanging underneath one end when swimming ashore or when awaiting rescue. If you turn it over, the cockpit will scoop up gallons of water, making it useless as a life-raft and very difficult to rescue and empty.

Exercises (Figs 33 & 34)

1. If you have two strong friends, a simple exercise will show you how easy it is to hold yourself in the boat with your knees when you are upsidedown. Your friends stand one at each end of the boat and you prepare yourself

for a capsize, with particular attention to hug ging the boat. As you go over, the boat is lifte right out of the water. Let go with your arm and just hang from your knees. It is muc easier than it looks, even though you ar holding your full body weight. In a real capsiz you will be underwater where your body almost weightless. (Make sure your frienc put you down gently.)

2. This is very simple, yet it will ensure tha you get used to forward-somersaulting fron the very first practice. Ask someone to stan alongside you and place whichever of h hands is nearest your back, so that it catche the back of your neck as you capsize towarc him. When you are upsidedown, this han pushes gently forward to force the forwar roll.

33 Gripping with your knees. This is a valuable training exercise as long as the 'lifters' and the boat are strong enough. Very lightweight boats should not be used, although Ricky's 9½ stone is no problem in this case. You can see that Nick and I are holding the boat in from the ends, not only taking any strain off them, but giving us better control.

34 Assisted exit upsidedown. If you have difficulty forward rolling out of the boat, a helping hand can get you used to the action. One is on the back of Spud's neck, pushing it forward and encouraging his exit in a perfect somersault.

Fig 35   Emptying the boat. The standard emptying routine is made easier by
          holding the boat in from the ends. This will enable you to keep it
          perfectly upsidedown. While David lifts, Darren has greater control, by
          resting the deck across his forearm.

Fig 36   Emptying a waterlogged boat. A special procedure is necessary when
          the boat is either too heavy to lift or where to do so would risk breaking
          it. The boat must be kept perfectly level and on its side, so that the
          water can run out of the cockpit. Both boys are wearing lifejackets
          (uninflated) and you can see the strap around David's waist, as well as
          the one keeping the collar away from his neck.

37 Solo emptying. Dominic can manage this alone by resting one end high up on the bank. Note the control he has with his arm under the boat.

EMPTYING THE BOAT
(Figs 35 to 37)

This is best undertaken by two people, one at each end. They can be either in or out of the water, as long as both can stand.

Leave the boat upsidedown.

If it has little or no water in it, it will be easy to lift with one person holding each end. An initial jerk may be necessary to break the suction between the cockpit and the water. Most of the water will come out as you lift, but the remainder can be emptied by each person alternately lifting and lowering his end.

3. If the boat has taken in a lot of water, do not try to lift it. Even if you are strong enough (unlikely, as a cubic metre of water weighs a tonne), the boat is not and it will be damaged. Carefully turn the boat on its side, not only so that you break the air seal of the cockpit with the water, but also that the water empties out of the cockpit sideways. Lift and rock the last few drops out as described above.

4. It is possible to empty the boat alone. Put one end onto the bank or something else higher than the water and lift the other end alternately above and below the level of it.

6 How Boats Behave

This chapter sets out to explain a little about why the kayak behaves as it does, but it is not essential reading before you go afloat for the first time. It will, however, give you a better understanding of what is happening to the boat and should be read as background material as you progress through the practical skills.

SPEED *(Figs 38 & 39)*

Have you noticed that whenever a duck wants to move fast, it leaves the water and flies? And whenever a seal wants to move fast, it dives and swims underwater? What these creatures do in common, is that they avoid staying partly in water and partly in air, a situation which severely restricts speed. Even speed-boats and hydrofoils do so by *planing*, a technique whereby a combination of design and power enables them to stay just on or above the surface. A kayak could have a similar design, but with you or I (or even both of us) it would have nothing like enough power.

The problem is created by the wave that comes from the front of the boat (bow-wave or wake) as you paddle along. Try as hard as you like, it is impossible to overtake it. In very simple terms, a boat generates a bow-wave with a length (the distance between one wave crest and the next) of about one metre, at your normal paddling speed, i.e. about 4½ kph. The kayak is likely to be 4 metres long, so you can expect four waves to be obvious along its length.

A law of physics means that as your speed increases, the wavelength increases twice as fast. In other words, if you double your speed to 9 kph (almost impossible), the wavelength will increase fourfold, i.e. 4 metres. Your 4 metre long boat will now sit perfectly in the trough between two waves. The only way out of this situation is to maintain your speed and find the extra energy to climb the slope of the wave – impossible. The same problem applies to the duck and the seal, so one flies and the other dives.

MOVEMENT *(Fig 40)*

Movement in any direction is the result of the boat moving along or around one of three imaginary lines. Each line is called an axis and they exist:

1. Down through the middle (vertical axis).
2. Across the width (short axis).
3. Along the length (long axis).

Any progress is made by moving along the long axis (forwards or backwards) or along the short axis (sideways). Any turning or loss of balance is the result of moving around an axis around the long axis for loss of balance, and around the vertical axis for turning.

Progress, or movement along an axis, is normally the result of deliberate forwards backwards or sideways paddling action. Turning and loss of balance, however, may be deliberate or accidental. For instance, when you are paddling forwards (along the long axis) your technique may not be perfect and the boat starts to turn to one side (around the vertical axis), or you may come across some

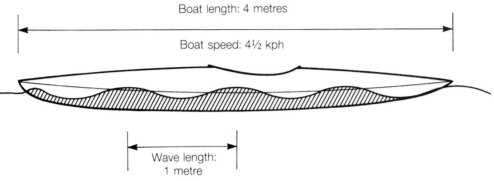

Boat length: 4 metres

Boat speed: 4½ kph

Wave length:
1 metre

* g 38   An illustration of a boat generating waves at one metre intervals when
travelling at approximately 4½ kph, i.e. normal paddling speed. The
4 metre boat is, therefore, supported by four waves.*

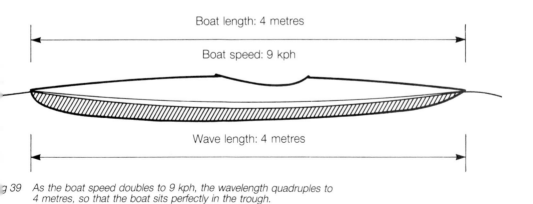

Boat length: 4 metres

Boat speed: 9 kph

Wave length: 4 metres

*g 39   As the boat speed doubles to 9 kph, the wavelength quadruples to
4 metres, so that the boat sits perfectly in the trough.*

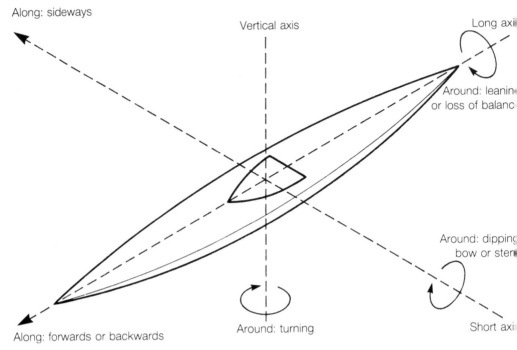

Along: sideways

Vertical axis

Long axis

Around: leaning or loss of balance

Around: dipping bow or stern

Around: turning

Short axis

Along: forwards or backwards

Fig 40   The three axes (or imaginary lines) along which and around which the boat can move. All movement is according to one or more of these possibilities.

rough water and lose your balance (around the long axis).

BOAT DESIGN

The design of a boat affects the ease or difficulty with which it will deliberately or accidentally move along or around one of its axes. Each different area of the sport (slalom, sprint, sea, etc) uses a kayak of a design that is best suited for speed or manoeuvrability or buoyancy or whatever is important. Unfortunately there is no perfect design, as what might be good for one type of movement may be bad for another.

Speed *(Fig 41)*

The longer a kayak, the faster it can travel. This is because the longer the boat, the faster it needs to travel before it generates two bow

waves far enough apart to be able to get caught in the trough between them. A narrow boat will cut easily through the water and be faster than a wide one. In addition, one with a semi-circular or V-shaped hull has less surface area in the water than one with a flat bottomed hull, produces less friction, and is therefore faster.

Course

The longer a boat, the better it will hold a straight course (along its long axis). A shorter boat has a tendency to veer off course (around its vertical axis). In addition, a boat with a V-shaped hull cross-section will dig deeper into the water and hold a better course than a flat-bottomed one. Bear in mind however, that the overall length of a kayak may not be the same as the length that is actually in the water (called the *waterline*). Some boats (notably pure slalom kayaks

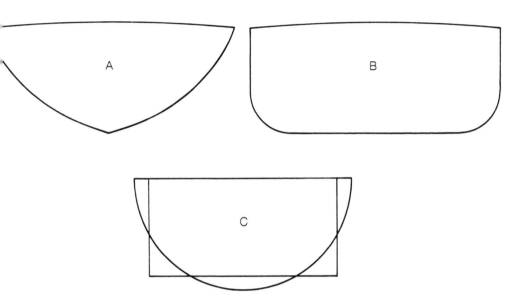

41　These shapes of a hull in cross-section help illustrate how differences affect performance. 'A' cuts down into the water and will hold a straighter course, although the roundness of its shape will make it a little unstable. 'B' will tend to skid across the water, but its flat bottom will make it more stable. 'A' is also faster than 'B' as, although they have the same width and depth, 'A' has less surface area than 'B'. 'C' proves this, being designs of identical area (and therefore buoyancy) superimposed on each other. Although the round shape appears larger it has over 11 per cent less surface area in the water. Less surface area creates less friction and enables the boat to travel faster.

...ve almost banana shaped hulls so that the ...ds are above the surface and only the ...ddle is in the water. This roundness along ...e length of the boat is called *rocker*.

...alance *(Fig 42)*

...e narrower the boat, the more likely it is to ...psize (around its long axis). Balance is, of ...urse, closely related to how much you lean. Everybody has a centre of gravity (CG), an ...aginary point that is approximately the cen-...e of the bulk and weight of your body. When ...u are standing, it is somewhere in your stomach area. As long as this point is kept above your feet, you are balanced. As soon as you lean and your CG is no longer directly above your feet, you are unstable and may fall over. A similar situation exists when you are canoeing, except that the boat has its own CG. Yours and the boat's must be one above the other for maximum stability; lean to one side and you become unstable.

Buoyancy *(Fig 43)*

This is related to the volume of the boat and governs the extent to which it can (deliberately

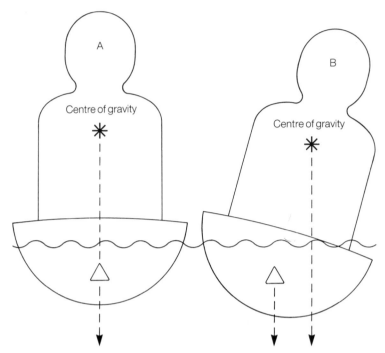

Fig 42 When your centre of gravity is above that of the boat, you are stable as in 'A'. If you lean, and your centre of gravity moves to one side of that of the boat, as in 'B', you become unstable and must use special strokes to prevent capsizing.

or accidentally) be made to sink at the front or back (around the short axis). The less volume in the front end (for instance), the easier it is to lean forward and dip the bow under a slalom gate, or the easier it can be for the boat to be made to dive into a wave.

STROKES

Low Strokes *(Fig 44)*

These are strokes where the paddle is kept as level and low over the water as possible. They enable you to reach away from the boat and apply more leverage around an axis. Low strokes are for:

1. Turning, i.e. movement around the vertical axis. The further the blade is from the boat, the greater the leverage that can be applied. The

blade itself is upright, as power must be applied towards the bow or stern as appropriate.
2. Supporting, i.e. movement around the long axis. This can prevent capsizing. The blade is flat on the water, as power must be applied downwards, in order to force the boat back up.

High Strokes *(Fig 45)*

These are strokes where the paddle is kept as near vertical as possible, in order to apply power along (or as close as possible to) the line of an axis. They are used for making progress forwards, backwards, or sideways.

Dynamic Strokes

A dynamic stroke is one in which you move the paddle in order to make the boat move. The propeller of a ship has a dynamic action

46

movement causing the ship to move. For-
ards, backwards, sideways and sweep
rokes are examples of dynamic strokes.

tatic Strokes

static stroke is one in which the boat is
oving and you can alter its course by holding
e paddle still in the water. The rudder of a
hip has a static action, its position being
fective only if the ship is moving. Bow and
ern rudders are examples of static strokes.

tatic Paddle Concept

luch as you might thrash your paddle about
the water to try to make your kayak do
hatever you want it to, nothing much will
appen.

If this sounds ridiculous, consider the most
common stroke of forward paddling. You are
sitting in the boat with the paddle poised
above the water, ready to put the blade into
the water and pull it along the side of the boat
with all the strength you can find. But if you just
pull the paddle along the side of the boat, the
boat will stay still. What you really need to do is
put the paddle in the water, leave it fixed there
and pull yourself and the boat up to and past
it. Think of your paddle as a post, but it must
not touch the bottom. It is the momentary
resistance of its surface area against the water
that will give you a few seconds of a reasonably fixed object on which to pull. When you
have the feel of this action, you will be sur-
prised by the improvement in the power and
effect of your strokes.

Fig 43   *(overleaf) Pearl-diving. This is what happens when a combination of
low volume boat, technique and suitable water make it possible for one
end (bow or stern) of the boat to be buried into a standing wave. Alan is
working on a fast-flowing mountain river, where the protection of a
crash helmet is essential.*

Fig 44   Low Stroke. The boat is moving around its long axis and Charlie is
          losing his balance. He is about to perform a hanging support stroke to
          correct the situation by moving the boat the other way around the
          same axis. The blade must be as far from the axis as possible so that
          maximum leverage can be applied. This requires keeping the whole
          paddle low (horizontal) over the water.

Fig 45   High Stroke. Nic is paddling forwards, thus moving the boat along its
          long axis. Ideally the blade should move along the axis, but that is not
          possible. By keeping the paddle high (almost vertical), however, it can
          be kept as close as possible.

50

Basic Strokes

fore looking at the individual strokes, it is cessary to be familiar with the general prin- ples of handling a paddle and the express- is used to explain its action.

OLDING THE PADDLE

ontrol Hand

hatever stroke you may be doing, one of ur hands (always the same one) will always p and the other will sometimes allow the aft to rotate in it. The hand that never anges its position is your *control hand* and knuckles must always be in line with the ade edge on the same side. Whether your ntrol hand is your right or left hand will rmally depend on how you have been ught, not necessarily whether you are right left handed. (Your control wrist, control arm control shoulder is, therefore, the wrist, arm shoulder driving the control hand.)

orrect Grip *(Fig 46)*

in the boat and hold the paddle shaft with th hands so that:

Your control hand knuckles are in line with blade edge.
The backs of both hands are uppermost.
They are at least as far apart as the width of cockpit. Their exact distance apart will be natter of personal choice, but too wide and ur reach is restricted, and too close and ur power (leverage) is reduced.
They are evenly spaced on the shaft, hav- ing the same amount of shaft on the right of the right hand as on the left of the left hand.

Front and Back of Blade

On flat blades there is no difference, only the way you hold the paddle determines which is which. If you hold the paddles correctly in front of you, the side of the blade facing you in your control hand is the front, sometimes called the *face*. For curved blades, the hollow side is the front and must be positioned to be so. Most of the time it is the front that provides the power against the water, although for the back- wards, stern and reverse strokes, the back of the blade is used. During your learning days, you will find it very helpful to mark the fronts of the blades, perhaps by putting stickers on them or painting them a different colour (*Fig 16*).

Left and Right

The explanations which follow never mention left or right. Continual reference can be con- fusing and would restrict the text to use by either right or left control-handed paddlers. Avoiding left and right is only possible by using the expressions such as control hand/arm/ shoulder, working blade (the one in the water), and top (highest) or bottom (lowest) hand. Whilst your control hand is always the same hand, your working blade and top and bottom hand alternate between being the right and left during the course of some strokes. If you are trying to copy a photograph and are con- fused because the subject is the other 'hand- edness' to you, hold the picture up to a mirror.

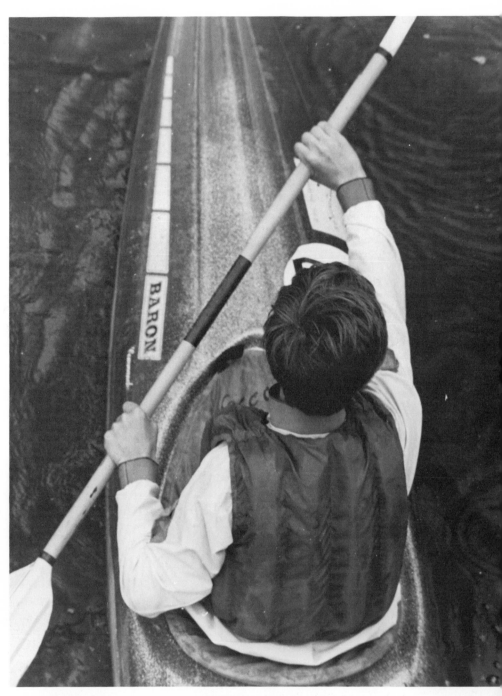

Fig 46 Paddle grip. There are many recommendations about how far your
hands should be apart, the answer depending on your size and what
feels comfortable and efficient. If the paddle is the correct length for
you, the best grip is often when each hand is about a quarter of a shaft
length away from each blade. Note that the knuckles of Nicholas'
control hand (right) are in line with the edge of the blade.

47 Forward stroke start. The bottom hand is reaching forward with the blade entering the water upright. The top hand is close to the shoulder, ready to push out. The body is leaning slightly forward, with the waist twisting the control shoulder even further forward. The paddle is high and is better seen in the head-on position in Fig 45.

his reverses the picture perfectly, including e fact that curved bladed paddles are set ther right or left handed.

ote

l the explanations which follow assume that ou have a correct paddle grip and a correct eating position, and only deal with the stroke n your control side. This is the easiest to erform when you are learning, but an early pportunity should be sought to practise on e other side.

It is not necessary to look at the blade in the ater. Whilst this may help at the outset, get ut of the habit as quickly as you can. Looking o and ahead will give you better control of the oat and lessen the chance of capsizing. You ould never think of looking at your feet when ou are walking!

FORWARD STROKE
(Figs 47 to 49)

This is the basic stroke for getting about, but is often neglected by beginners in favour of more stylish looking ones. It should, however, be carefully studied and practised.

Chapter 6 explains why it is that for this stroke to be perfect, the blade needs to move along the imaginary line along the centre of the boat. This is not possible, as you can only paddle on one side of the boat or the other. The slight turning effect that this produces can be kept to a minimum by using as perfect a technique as possible.

Fig 48   Forward stroke finish. The working blade is being lifted clear of the water at the hip as the top arm and its shoulder are extended forward ready for the non-control side stroke.

Technique

1. Twist from the waist so that your control shoulder turns forward, straighten your control arm and drop the control blade into the water. Your non-control arm should be bent with its hand in a position close to its shoulder. It is important that the blade enters the water as far forward as you can reach and close to the side of the boat.

2. Apply a pulling action to the control blade as soon as it is fully in the water, initially by untwisting your waist, but also by bending your control arm as soon as it is comfortable to do so. As you do this, move your non-control hand straight out from its position close to the shoulder, at the same time twisting the shoulder forward.

3. Your control blade will be in the water alongside your hips at the same time as your non-control arm is straight out in front of you and almost above the centre line of the kayak.

4. Lift the control blade out of the water (edge first so that it does not lift any water), by the action of both lifting your control arm and lowering your non-control hand.

5. Now comes the twist to compensate for feathered blades, and you will find the explanation easier to follow if you have marked the front of your blades as previously suggested. Your non-control blade is next to go into the water, but it is at the wrong angle. Lift your control hand up to shoulder height and bend (flex) its wrist back (upwards), at the same time loosening the grip of your non-control hand to allow the shaft to rotate.

6. Regrip your non-control hand once the blade has turned through 90°, and it will be ready to go into the water.

7. Drop the non-control blade into the water (close to the side and well forward as before) your control hand taking up a position close to its shoulder.

49 Wrist flexing. Alan paddles right control hand, and his wrist is flexing back to allow the non-control blade to be at the correct angle in the water.

Execute the stroke with your non-control
ide.
Your control wrist remains flexed all
'ough its moving out from the shoulder,
urning to normal (and allowing the shaft to
ate in the non-control hand) just before the
ntrol blade goes back into the water.

ults

Not keeping the blade close enough to the
Je of the boat, with the paddle high.
Not holding the paddle evenly.
Not putting each blade in the water at the
me angle.
Not taking the blade out of the water when
s alongside your hips.
Not looking straight ahead.
Trying to correct any turning by a back-
ards stroke. Having put all your energy into
oving forwards, there is no use in paddling

backwards. Follow the advice under the section on sweep strokes.

Exercises (Fig 50)

1. If you find it difficult flexing your control
wrist, you can practise on dry land and con-
centrate on the technique without having to
worry about the boat. Hold the paddle in front
of you and get an experienced paddler to
stand behind you with his arms around the
outside of you. He can hold your hands, forcing the control hand to flex and the other to
relax as appropriate.
2. Practise keeping the boat on a straight
course by following the first exercise under the
forward sweep stroke.
3. Develop the static paddle concept. Use
shallow water, so that you can keep the paddle still by digging it into the river bed, and get
used to the action of pulling the boat past it.

Fig 50 Dry paddling. A beginner can benefit greatly from having experienced hands guiding from behind. I have mine over Ricky's, forcing his control (top) hand to flex back while relaxing the fingers of the other to allow the shaft to spin.

3. The restrictions of your shoulder joints d not allow you to keep the paddle high whil it is behind you. The stroke, therefore, star low and becomes higher as it progresse although rarely as high as the forward strok

4. Look where you are going by glancing ov your shoulder from time to time. It is advisab always to look over the same shoulder, th control side normally being the most comfor able.

5. Whilst it is possible to keep the workir blade close to the boat, this often results in th power being applied downwards, rather tha along. A more effective action comes fro keeping the blade 30cm to 40cm from th side.

6. Although it is important to take the blad out of the water alongside the hips, it is not a critical as in the forward stroke.

Faults

1. Lowering the paddles too much so th your movement becomes a series of turnir strokes.

2. Not looking where you are going.

BACKWARD STROKE
(Fig 51)

This is almost the reverse action of the forward stroke, but there are some important differences. The main difference results from your body's inability to work well at the back of the boat whilst sitting facing forward.

Technique

1. Do not alter your grip on the paddle, as the stroke uses the back of the blade for power.

2. In order to get the paddle in the water as far back as possible, you will need to lean back and twist from the waist.

STOPPING STROKE

This is most often used in the sense of a emergency stop, and is essentially paddlin backwards to stop yourself going forward and vice versa.

Technique

1. The stopping stroke differs from the nor mal power stroke, in that if you are paddlin forwards at great speed and need to stop, t dig a blade in the water suddenly for a powe ful backwards stroke may either snap off th blade, dislocate your shoulder, or capsiz you.

1   Backwards paddling. Whilst this should be a high stroke, the
limitations of body movement do not allow it to be high at the start.
Note how much twist is necessary to get the blade as far back as
possible and that Nic is looking where he is going.

Fig 52 *Stopping practice. The stopping stroke can put considerable strain on paddle and paddler. The extent to which the body contributes (static paddle concept) can be felt by pulling yourself backwards and forwards on a paddle held across the boat. Martin and Nicholas have to hold tight, as the force of Charlie suddenly stopping his backwards movement is bending the shaft.*

2. The answer is to do the stroke with only part of the blade immersed. Because of the reduced amount of blade in the water, it will have reduced power. To compensate, it is necessary for stopping strokes to be performed in very rapid succession.

3. Any instability created by the stopping action is corrected by *flattening out* the blade a little. This is explained further under recovery strokes.

Faults

1. Digging the blade in too deep.
2. Not paddling fast enough.
3. Not bracing yourself in the boat.

Exercises (Fig 52)

1. Get used to the feel of sudden braking by asking two friends to hold a paddle across the front of you. Hold on to the shaft as normal and move the boat vigorously forwards and backwards with your body. The quick change in direction will put quite a strain on you and on your grip in the boat.

2. Work to and fro across a narrow river between two fixed points. Paddle fast forwards to one point, stop, then paddle fast backwards to the other. With practice you will be able to stop in a matter of centimetres and with a minimum number of strokes.

ORWARD SWEEP TROKE *(Fig 53)*

is is a turning stroke, and understanding it
s cope with the unintentional turning that
urs in forward paddling. The two strokes
usefully be studied together.

he stroke turns the bow away from the
rking blade or stops an unintentional turn
vards it. The boat may be stationary or
ving. Chapter 6 explains why it is neces-
y to keep the blade as far away from the
tre of the boat as possible.

echnique

Reach forwards with your control arm,
ing your control shoulder with it and lean-
your body further forwards. The paddle
uld be low and your non-control hand
se to your lower chest.

Put the blade in the water so that it is
ight.

Keep your control arm straight and sweep
blade to a position directly off your side,
aightening out your non-control arm (top
) a little as you do so. At the same time,
st your shoulders back to their normal posi-
and sit upright. This movement utilises the
y strong muscles in your waist and back to
nsmit more power into the stroke.

Continue the sweep to a position as far
ck as possible. To achieve this, your non-
ntrol arm reaches across the boat and
aightens, your body leans back and your
ntrol shoulder turns towards the stern.

Lift the control blade out of the water be-
e it reaches the side of the boat. If it goes
far, the blade has a tendency to go under-
ath the boat and lead to a capsize.

Do not lean the kayak at all.

After one complete stroke, your boat may
ve turned over half a circle. Its exact turning

ability is determined by its design.

Faults

1. Not sweeping from as far forward to as far back.
2. Not reaching out as far as possible (with-out leaning) by keeping the bottom arm straight and the paddle low.
3. Not using the leaning forwards, back-wards and twisting of your body.
4. Not having the blade completely im-mersed.

Exercises *(Fig 54)*

1. Deliberately let the boat wander off course during forward paddling and bring in a sweep stroke to correct the error. It may not be necessary to do a full correction stroke, simply lowering the paddle and reaching out a little may be sufficient.
2. Develop the static paddle concept by get-ting a friend to hold a blade, rather than you put it in the water. Do a full sweep stroke concentrating on the powerful muscles of your body turning the boat via your knees. Mastering this body action will dramatically improve your stroke.

REVERSE SWEEP STROKE

This is the exact reverse of the forward sweep stroke, with the paddle moving from stern to bow and the bow turning towards the blade. As in all backwards paddling, it is not neces-sary to alter your grip on the paddles, as the back of the blade applies the power.

Exercises

1. Practise both forward and reverse sweep

Fig 53 Forward sweep stroke. The low nature of this stroke can be clearly
seen, with Rob leaning forward and turning his working shoulder
forward to get the blade in the water (upright) as near the bow as
possible.

54 Sweep stroke practice. This simple practice routine allows you to feel the effect of the static paddle concept in the forwards or reverse stroke. Have a friend hold your working blade 'static', while you make your body and arm action move the boat.

rokes on your non-control side. It is impor-nt from the point of view of mastering the rist flexing, as well as to ensure that both des of your body develop equally in strength nd technique.

Do a forward sweep on one side and, as ou lift the blade out of the water, stay leaning ack and put the other blade in the water on s side to do a reverse sweep. The combina-on of one forward and one reverse stroke ll, with correct paddle and body action, turn ost modern kayaks more than a complete rcle.

IDEWAYS STROKE

igs 55 & 56)

his is normally called the *draw* stroke, on ccount of the boat being drawn through the ater. The sideways movement may be re-uired to move your boat alongside a jetty or

other canoeist, or out of the way of an ob-stacle. Chapter 6 explains why the paddle should be kept as vertical as possible and moved along an imaginary line drawn through your hips.

Technique

1. The correct starting position is with one arm stretched out sideways with its blade in the water, front facing you. An easy way to learn this position is:
(a) hold the paddle correctly in front of you;
(b) straighten both arms;
(c) lift the paddle above your head, keeping your arms straight;
(d) swing your arms sideways until the control blade is in the water.

2. Your top hand (non-control hand) should now be in front of your face and the shaft at an angle of about 45°. You may lean the boat a

Fig 55   Sideways (draw) stroke start. The stroke starts with the bottom arm
reaching out from the hip, leaning a little to get even more reach. Note
that Chris is looking ahead. Looking at the blade makes you feel
unstable and go off course.

56 Sideways (draw) stroke finish. The stroke finishes close to the boat and
    high. Amelia is leaning slightly away from the paddle, a position that
    has to be adopted as soon as the stroke starts, so that the gunwale
    does not dig into the water and cause a capsize. Note that she is
    looking straight ahead, although her shoulders are still turned towards
    the paddle.

Basic Strokes

little in order to get a better reach.

3. Pull on your bottom hand so that the blade moves directly towards your hip, and push your top hand towards the opposite shoulder, until its arm is across the front of you. At the same time, twist your waist so that your chest turns towards the paddle.

4. Whilst doing this, you must change the lean of the boat to being away from the blade in the water. This will let the boat skim easily over the water and lessen the risk of capsizing towards the paddle.

5. The stroke finishes with the paddle as near vertical as possible and the blade in the water about 20cm from the boat. You should be able to look forward over your top shoulder or arm.

6. If you need to return the blade to its starting position for a second stroke, try not to lift it out of the water. It is better to flex your bottom wrist forwards (the opposite way to normal paddling) and slice the blade back to the starting position edge first.

Faults

1. Not pulling on the bottom hand and pushing on the top hand at the same time.
2. Not drawing the blade towards your hip, whilst keeping it parallel to the boat.
3. Not bringing the paddle to an upright position early in the stroke, probably by not turning the chest towards the working blade as you pull yourself towards it.
4. Not leaning away from the working blade immediately after the stroke has started.

Exercises

1. The static paddle concept is easy to practise by choosing some shallow water and jamming the working blade on the bottom.
2. Choose an open and calm stretch of water and turn the boat to face the bank or shore.

Practise the draw stroke, looking ahead ov your top arm to see that you are stayir square to the bank. If you draw the blade slightly behind your hips, you will find that th stern moves out a bit. Conversely, if you dra the blade in more towards your knees you w move the bow out. These movements enab you to steer an exact course.

3. Practise the stroke leaning towards th blade slightly and then leaning away. Th latter should be noticeably faster and mo stable.

RECOVERY STROKE
(Fig 57)

This stroke gives you a split second of suppo whilst you recover your balance. Chapter explains why the paddle should be kept lov over the water and the working blade as fa away from you as possible.

Technique

When the boat feels unstable:

1. Reach the arm out on the side toward which the boat is tipping.
2. Flex the wrist forwards so that the back c the blade can be placed flat on the water.
3. Push down smartly on the back of th blade and use the resistance of the water t push your body and boat into balance again

Faults

1. Not getting the back of the blade flat on th water.
2. Not reaching out from the boat.
3. Not making the downward pressure on th blade fast enough.

ercises

The blade will only momentarily keep its
istance on the water, during which time
ur balance needs to be regained. Develop
body movement by resting the working
de on a bank or friend's boat so that it
nnot sink.

During normal paddling, just as the work-
blade is leaving the water, lean towards it a
e. You should react immediately by
ching out and flattening out the blade onto
back. Do this on one side after the other
il your confidence grows and the amount
lean increases. With practice you will be
e to get the edge of the cockpit under
ter.

3. Ask a friend to stand in the water and hold
on to the back of your boat. He can tip the
boat to one side or the other, with you reacting
accordingly.

THE RAFT *(Fig 58)*

This is not a stroke, but an important technique for keeping a group of canoeists together. It can be useful when an instructor
wants to address everybody at the same
time and invaluable for keeping everybody
together as a safety measure. In addition, the
raft can be such a stable platform, that a
paddler can get out of his boat onto the decks
of the others, possibly to stretch his legs or

57 Recovery stroke. The action of the back of the blade being pushed
down on the water can correct a slight loss of balance. Note that
Justine's wrists are flexed forwards to achieve this, the right (control)
one still having its knuckles in line with the edge of the blade.

Basic Strokes

even repair his boat. To form a raft, all the paddlers come together side by side and facing the same way, with each person holding the cockpit of the boat on either side of him. The paddle is best laid diagonally across the cockpit and under one arm. If one end of the raft is not anchored by a paddler holding onto the bank, those on either end may need to do some strokes in order to stop the whole thing drifting or turning.

Fig 58 • Rafting. A group of absolute beginners have been brought together so that one can get out of his boat and stretch his legs. The instructor, Carol, can remain apart from the raft and direct proceedings. She has positioned a more experienced person on each end to stop the raft drifting or turning in the wind. Note that the paddles do not need to be held, but are ready for immediate use. The practice of laying them across everybody's laps is cumbersome and should be restricted to situations where increased stability is required.

Advanced Strokes

ese strokes will enable you to cope with a riety of situations, but do not move onto em until you have a good command of all the sic ones. It is assumed that you will have rned to use, and be wearing, a spraydeck.

round and Water Speed

is important to understand the difference tween these as some strokes (static okes) do not work without water speed. Let us assume you paddle at 5 kph. On lm water, this will be your speed through the ater (water speed) as well as your speed ative to the river bed or bank (ground eed). On moving water, however, the situa- n is different. If the current is flowing at 2 kph d you paddle against it, your water speed l still be 5 kph, but your ground speed will only 3 kph. Against a current of 5 kph, you l be paddling hard but making no progress, . no ground speed. Against a current of kph, your ground speed will be 2 kph back- ards! If you drift you have no water speed d a ground speed equal to the speed of the rrent.

TERN RUDDER *(Fig 59)*

is stroke steers the boat by moving the ck of it and forcing the front to change its urse. It is a static stroke, requires water eed and has a slight braking effect. It is quently used to hold a course in surf or to er through narrow rocky passages.

Technique

1. Extend your control arm behind you, turn- ing the control shoulder (and even leaning back slightly) as you do so.
2. Place the blade upright in the water with the front facing the side of the boat, as for the start of the reverse sweep stroke.
3. The paddle should be kept low, with your non-control hand alongside your waist on your control side.
4. The angle of the blade to the boat deter- mines how quickly or slowly the boat turns. Parallel to the boat, the blade has almost no effect.
5. The angle can be altered during the stroke, although (technically speaking) any move- ment may turn the action into part of a sweep stroke.

Faults

1. Not reaching back far enough.
2. Not finding the correct angle between the blade and the boat to produce the action required.
3. Not bracing your knees and feet to trans- mit the steering action.

Exercises

1. On a flat stretch of water, paddle forwards to obtain good speed and a straight course. Put the paddle in the water parallel to the length of the boat and the steering effect will be minimal. Increase the angle between the blade and the boat and the steering effect will be felt. Practise quickly, as the boat soon

Fig 59   Stern rudder. This is a static stroke with the blade held at an angle
close to the stern. Note that Charlie achieves this by twisting his waist
and leaning and reaching back, as well as having almost the entire
paddle on the working side.

ws down once you stop paddling. Different
I designs will react differently, rounded hulls
ning faster than V-shaped ones.

Try to get the opportunity to practise in
f. Sitting in your boat, position yourself a
v yards off-shore, facing directly inland.
ien a wave comes up behind you, paddle
wards and it will lift the back of your boat
d push you towards the shore. You are
likely to go straight ahead for long, as the
at will start to turn (called *broaching*). Im-
ediately do a stern rudder on the side away
m which the boat is turning. This should
ng you back onto a straight course for the
ore.

OW DRAW

is stroke moves the bow towards the blade,
us turning the boat on its vertical axis. It is a
namic stroke and is used extensively in
ilom work and for breaking-in and breaking-
t of moving water.

echnique

Place the paddle as if to start a normal
aw stroke, but flex your bottom wrist back
that the front of the blade faces the front of
e boat.

Keep your bottom arm almost straight and
sh the blade forwards and inwards towards
e bow. Sit forward as you do so, bringing the
werful muscles of your trunk into play.

Move your top hand across your face and
ish the stroke with the blade fairly close to
e boat. Take care not to get the top blade or
p hand caught at the back of the head.

aults

Not starting the stroke as far out as you
n reach.

2. Not keeping a good hold with both hands,
particularly in the last half of the stroke.
3. Not using the muscles of your trunk by
leaning forward during the stroke.

Exercises

1. At the end of the stroke, flex the bottom
wrist forwards so that the blade can be sliced
back to its starting position out from your hips.
Sit up as you do so. Repeat the stroke over
and over again without taking the blade out of
the water.
2. Develop the static paddle concept by
being in water shallow enough for the blade to
touch the bottom.

BOW RUDDER *(Fig 60)*

This stroke alters the course of the boat by
steering the bow and letting the rest of the
boat follow. It is a static stroke, requires water
speed and has a braking effect.

Technique

1. When you have water speed, plant the
blade in the water in the same position as the
end of the bow draw stroke, but with the front
of the blade turned a little forwards. This involves considerable arm and wrist twisting.
2. The blade often snatches as it goes into
the water, and you may find it helps to brace
your top wrist against your forehead. It would
be very dangerous, however, to let your top
blade get behind your neck or your top wrist
get across your throat.
3. The speed of the turn can be adjusted by
changing the angle of the blade to the boat. A
wide angle has a severe braking effect.

Fig 60   Bow rudder. This stroke has all the characteristics of the stern rudder, but with the blade at an angle to the bow of the boat. Note that Nic's top arm is braced on his forehead, not across his throat or behind his head.

61 Hip-flick practice. I am holding a paddle, so that it can be used like the
rail of a swimming pool. This technique puts me in a good position to
control the situation and enables me to feel how much pressure is
being applied to the bar. Ricky has flicked the boat up with his hips, has
his body following, and is starting to lean back to lower his centre of
gravity.

ROSS BOW RUDDER

This is similar to the bow rudder, but is less
stable and therefore less popular. It is, however, an excellent exercise in trunk rotation,
blade awareness and general confidence.
The technique is the same as the bow rudder
stroke, except that the control blade goes into
the water on the non-control side of the boat
(or vice versa). The front of the blade should
still face forwards and care taken to ensure
that neither shaft nor arm locks across the
throat or behind the neck (Fig 64).

HIP-FLICK (Fig 61)

This is not a stroke, but a technique that is
essential for advanced support strokes (as

well as for eskimo rolling and eskimo rescue
techniques). It is a body movement that can
right the boat after a near or full capsize. To
recover your balance, your natural instinct will
be to try and push your body up first, but there
is seldom enough support to take your full
weight. The body is therefore left in the water
and the boat flicked up first.

Learning to Hip-flick

1. Position yourself alongside a fixed object
that you can hold comfortably with both
hands. The rail on the side of a swimming pool
or a paddle shaft held level with the water by
someone is ideal.
2. Take hold with both hands, grip well with
your knees and capsize the boat, without
letting go of the bar.

Fig 62   Hanging support stroke. Richard has capsized almost completely and
brought down the front of the blade firmly onto the water. Its resistance
is sufficient for a quick hip-flick. Note that the paddle is as low as
possible, with the bottom arm extended for maximum leverage. See
also Fig 44.

3. Bend your body so that your head comes
up towards the surface, leave your head there
and flick the boat upright with your knees,
using power from your waist and hips.

4. It will help if you lower your centre of gravity
immediately after you hip-flick, either by leaning forwards or backwards across the deck.

5. When you get the timing and action of the
flick perfect, the boat rights with such ease
that the body follows naturally.

Faults

1. Not gripping tight with your knees.

2. Not pulling yourself in slightly towards
whatever you are holding. (If your arms
straighten, your body will be stretched and not
flexible enough to flick properly.)

3. Not being supple in the waist.

4. Not leaving your head low until it is dra
ged up by your body action.

HANGING SUPPORT STROKE (Fig 62)

This is used to prevent a capsize, but (unlik
the recovery stroke) it can be used when th
kayak is completely off balance.

Technique

1. By bending your arms, bring the paddle t
a position in front of (and almost touching) th
top of your chest. The control blade now ha
its face downwards.

Extend your control arm out sideways until ur non-control hand is close to the control oulder.

Lean your body to take the boat off bal-ce, but keep the paddle parallel to the water you go over. This will involve lifting your control hand a little so that you are hanging nderneath.

At the point when you want to recover your alance, press the blade firmly down on the ater, and hip-flick off the resistance.

aults

Not having the blade flat (and front down) the water.

Not keeping the paddle low and reaching t.

Not hip-flicking properly.

langing versus Recovery

ou will see that the recovery stroke is on the ack of the blade and you are above the addle, whilst the hanging support stroke is the front and you are hanging underneath. oth enable you to recover any loss of bal-nce, something which normally arises sud-enly during the course of an otherwise ordin-y stroke. If the working blade is then in front f you, it is normally easier to turn it front down r a hanging support stroke; whereas if it is ehind you, it is easier to turn it back down for recovery stroke.

culling

his is a movement of the blade that can be troduced during the draw stroke (to become e sculling draw stroke) or during the hanging support stroke (to become the sculling sup-port stroke). Its action allows the blade to work during the entire stroke, unlike the ordin-ary stroke where the blade is ineffective whilst it is being returned to its starting position for a subsequent action.

SCULLING SUPPORT STROKE *(Fig 63)*

If, in the hanging stroke, your hip-flick does not work first time, the blade will sink before a second attempt is possible. The action of the sculling however, involves the blade moving backwards and forwards on the surface of the water and providing lift all the time.

Technique

1. Put the blade in the hanging support posi-tion on the water, but do not lean.
2. Tilt the front edge of the blade up a little and skim the blade across the surface to-wards the front of the boat. You will feel the blade lift onto the surface.
3. Once the paddle is well to the front of you, twist the blade through its front-down position and further on until the back edge tilts up a little. Sweep the paddle back with the blade lifting onto the surface as before.
4. Practise until the wrist action comes nat-urally, then lean on the stroke a little. You will find you can increase the lift of the blade by increasing its angle to the water.
5. After gaining confidence, you will be able to lay on the water supporting yourself entirely from this stroke.
6. Hip-flick to come up again.

Fig 63   *Sculling action. The blade is moving from right to left, the upturned leading edge making it lift and stay on the surface. This is the basis of all sculling, whether the blade is low with the leading edge up (e.g. sculling support stroke) or high with the leading edge out (e.g. sculling draw stroke).*

SCULLING DRAW STROKE

The blade action is the same as that of the sculling support stroke, except that the paddle is held high rather than low.

Technique

1. Adopt the start position for the ordinary draw stroke, but with the blade only about 35cm from the side of the boat, the body well twisted to the control side and the paddle almost vertical.

2. Flex your control wrist back so that the front edge of the blade is further away from the boat and move the blade towards the front of the boat, directly along an imaginary line parallel to the boat. You will feel the blade bite

in the water and a corresponding sideway movement of the boat towards it.

3. When the blade is approximately level with your knees, stop, twist it back to being parall to the boat and further on until the back edge is turned away from you. Move the blade bac along its imaginary line to a position behin you. The boat should continue to move.

4. Your first attempts may result in the bo and stern moving out one after the othe rather than a perfect sideways movement.

5. You will be able to alter your speed b increasing the angle of the blade to the boa

BRACING STROKES

There are occasions when you need to support yourself, not in water that is moving along but in water that is moving up inside a wave. It happens in stopper waves and in surf (*Fig 88*).

Technique

The paddle position is that of a recovery or a hanging support stroke. The difference is that the support strokes are dynamic, but the bracing strokes are static, i.e. the bracing stroke is held still whilst the water comes up to meet it. The action may be either a *low brace* (on the back of the blade) or a *hanging brace* (on the front of the blade). The decision as to which will depend on your paddle position at the moment of instability (see 'Hanging versus recovery') and the height of the wave.

LEANING TO TURN

This has two meanings:

1. A kayak will normally turn faster if you lean during a turning stroke, because you often shorten its waterline. A 4m kayak floating level may have a waterline of 3.80m. But the same boat on its side (because the curvature along its side is greater than along its hull) may have a waterline of only 3.40m (See Chapter 6).
2. A kayak being paddled forwards normally may turn if you lean. This is because the curvature of the hull and that of the deck are often different, but a bit of each will be in the water if you lean it on its side. The boat will then normally turn to the deck side or the hull side, according to which has the least roundness.

Exercises

It is important to know these two turning characteristics in your own boat, as they could significantly affect its performance, particularly in moving water. The former one can be researched by leaning your boat towards and away from the paddle during a sweep stroke and comparing turning performance. The latter can be demonstrated by paddling forwards, stopping the stroke and leaning to one side. The boat will turn one way or the other, but take care that your last paddle stroke does not influence the direction of the turn.

COMBINATION STROKES *(Fig 64)*

A combination stroke is the running together of two or more single strokes to form a continuous action. The component strokes are normally performed with one blade, which remains in the water.

You are already using combination strokes without realising it. When paddling forward and straying off course a little, you include a correcting sweep in the middle of the forward action.

There are many well-known combinations, one of the most popular being the Colorado Hook. It is a way of changing the course of one of the bulkier river boats from moving forward in one direction to moving forward in completely the opposite. (The more modern slalom boats will turn almost a complete circle on a single sweep stroke.)

Technique

1. The cross bow rudder. This will turn the bow sharply, and slow you down. As the stroke is ineffective without water speed, then;

Fig 64 *Cross bow rudder. This has a powerful turning effect, either as a stroke in its own right or in combination with others to form the Colorado Hook. It is also a good exercise in knee-bracing, trunk rotation and balance. The stroke is simply a bow rudder with the working blade working on the opposite side of the boat.*

2. The reverse sweep with support, achieved by flattening out the reverse stroke onto the back of the blade, in order to support you as you lean to accelerate the turn. When your extended bottom arm is at right angles to your hip, flex your wrist back for;

3. The bow draw. At about the start of this stroke the boat will have become stationary and you will be turning on the spot. As the blade comes into the bow, do;

4. The forward stroke and you should be travelling back along your original course.

9 Rolling

This is more correctly termed Eskimo rolling, having been developed by these arctic people. They would create a spraydeck by lacing the edge of a sealskin jacket to the rim of the cockpit, making getting out after a capsize almost impossible. In addition, the temperature of the water was such that prolonged immersion would have been fatal. The answer was to develop a technique that would right the boat without getting out. It is therefore self-rescue and is a combination of body and paddle movement. There are many different forms of the roll, but only a few of the basic ones are outlined here.

General

Technique

For all this may seem complex, all paddle rolls are a form of either the sculling or hanging support stroke started from a completely upsidedown position. A spraydeck is essential.

Disorientation

This is a loss of sense of direction, experienced in particular when you are hanging upsidedown in your boat. You will get over it much faster if you are able to see when underwater, either by wearing swimming goggles or a snorkeller's face-mask. Apart from general vision, you will also be able to see the paddle and its position, but stop using goggles as soon as you have acquired the basic technique.

Nose

The amount of time that you will inevitably spend underwater in practice, will cause a lot of water to go up your nose. It is uncomfortable, but easy to prevent, either by wearing a nose-clip or the face-mask referred to earlier.

Hip-flick

Whilst paddle rolls can be completed without a hip-flick, it puts a strain on the paddler's shoulders and expects a lot of the blade's resistance to the water. A well-timed hip-flick is therefore essential and an excellent hip-flick can enable a canoeist to roll with no paddle at all.

Buoyancy

Almost any clothing you wear contains some air and will create drag in the water, especially in the case of your buoyancy aid. This can upset your early rolling attempts and you may choose to discard any guilty garments. Only do so in well controlled and supervised situations, and put everything on again as soon as you have the basic technique.

Bar Rolling

The bar may be the rail on the edge of a swimming pool or a friend standing alongside you holding a paddle level with the water (*Fig 61*). The technique gives you the feel of capsizing on one side and coming up on the other, without the problem of handling your

Rolling

own paddle. It is therefore a valuable orientation exercise.

Hold on to the bar with both hands and practise a few ordinary hip-flicks. Then move your boat close alongside the bar and capsize away from it. Put your hands up to the bar from underwater, take hold of it, hip-flick and you are up again.

You may need some assistance during your first attempts, by means of a helper pushing your boat back to within reach of the bar, and then directing your hands to it. As you become proficient, practise by coming up holding with one hand only. The easiest hand to use is the one nearest the bar before you capsize. Then try it with the other hand only.

Canoe Swimming *(Fig 65)*

This will also help overcome disorientation, as well as increase your confidence in being upsidedown and wearing a spraydeck. It is a way of swimming whilst still in the boat and can be used either to swim a few metres to safety or to come up for air between failed rolls.

Capsize, grip tight with your knees and bring your body to the surface by laying backwards and turning to one side. Then swim, the best stroke being a breast stroke action with a little downward pressure on each stroke to give you lift.

Fig 65   Canoe swimming. This is about the only skill that is best practised wearing only swimwear, as the lack of buoyancy from any canoe clothing makes it more difficult to get to the surface to breathe. To do so, Dominic has to force his breast stroke action slightly downwards to give extra lift, and then turn his head so that his face breaks the surface.

Fig 66   Pawlata roll wind-up (LH). Nick's control hand keeps its knuckles in line with the edge of the blade, and is no more than half way forward along the shaft. The wind-up is clear with both wrists flexed strongly forward so as to tilt the working blade for its sculling action during the roll. Note that the non-working blade is alongside the hip.

If you find it difficult to get your head out of the water to breathe, don't panic. Simply twist your neck, thus turning your face upwards to break the surface for air.

It is easiest to swim to a point slightly behind you and the whole technique is not a difficult one as long as you relax. If you are tense, your body will not be supple enough, and if you panic and thrash about in the water, you will quickly use up precious oxygen and need to breathe more frequently.

Your Handedness

Mention was made in the chapter on basic strokes regarding any confusion that the photographs might create, if you are the other handedness to the subject. This is of particular importance for the rolling photographs that follow. Remember that if you paddle right

control hand and the photograph is demonstrating a left control handed roll (or vice versa), holding the picture up to a mirror will reverse it perfectly. To help you further, all the captions to the pictures are marked RH (right handed) or LH (left handed) according to the style and the paddle being used.

PAWLATA ROLL
(Figs 66 & 67)

This roll necessitates moving the hands from the normal position, in order to give extra leverage. It should be used as a stepping stone to the other rolls, as they require no hand moving, and be reserved thereafter for situations where tiredness or difficult water conditions demand a roll with extra power. It is a forward roll, in that you start by leaning

Rolling

forward with the paddle towards the front of the boat.

Technique

1. Hold the paddle normally but slide the control hand along to the middle of the shaft. Check that your knuckles are still in line with the blade edge.

2. Lay the paddle on the water along the non-control side of the boat, with the back of the control blade on the surface and the non-control blade alongside your hip.

3. Let go with your non-control hand and reposition it on the outside (front) of the bottom corner of the non-control blade. If it is

necessary to slide your control hand nearer you to achieve this position, then do so b remain leaning forward.

4. Flex the control wrist forwards so that tl control blade no longer lies flat, but is angl down and away from you. This is call winding-up the paddle, is uncomfortable hold, but essential if the blade is to sc correctly during the roll.

5. Capsize, keeping the paddle tight again the side of the boat. The control blade will ju break the surface on the other side.

6. With your control arm straight, sweep past your face. At the same time push forwa with your non-control hand, sit up and hi flick.

Fig 67   Pawlata roll sweep (LH). The roll must not start until the working blade breaks the surface at the side of the boat. Once the sweep has started, the non-control hand (holding the blade) is better able to keep the paddle wound-up, thus tilting the leading edge of the working blade. Reaching out for the sweeping/sculling action makes the body float to the surface, and the lift of the working blade provides enough resistance for a good hip-flick.

g 68 Assisted rolling preparation (RH). So that beginners never get into bad habits, an instructor should start by guiding the paddle through its entire movement. By reaching under the boat, I can hold the paddle in the correct position and with maximum wind-up, to ensure that Ricky starts the roll properly.

Faults

. Not leaning forward.

. Not flexing the control wrist.

. Not keeping paddle alongside boat during capsize.

. Not capsizing completely before starting the roll.

. Not keeping control arm straight and close to your face.

. Not hip-flicking when the blade has resistance against the water.

. Manoeuvring the paddle incorrectly due to disorientation.

Exercises (Figs 68 & 69)

It will help enormously to have an instructor standing alongside in the water. He can hold and guide the paddle from a point before you even capsize. It is possible for someone in another kayak, positioned across the front of you, to guide the blade.

A half-roll may be found useful. Position yourself as if you are going to capsize and roll, but capsize to your control side. It is possible to start the roll before your head has gone underwater, so that there is no disorientation.

Simulate a real situation by capsizing whilst paddling along and finding the start position whilst upsidedown.

Remember that the roll is a form of sculling support stroke. If you are not up by the time the blade has sculled to the stern, flex your wrist back and scull to the front, trying to hip-flick up as you do so.

Fig 69   Assisted rolling execution (RH). During the roll itself, an instructor can
         exercise absolute control over the sweeping motion and the wind-up,
         as well as sense the effort and technique being applied by the learner.

Fig 70   Screw roll wind-up (LH). With the hands unchanged from the normal
         paddling position, Nick prepares for a screw roll. Compare the position
         with that of the Pawlata roll in Fig 66.

Fig 71   Screw roll sweep (LH). By the time the blade has sculled its way to a
position at 90° to the boat, you should be nearly up. With his working
blade still providing lift, Nick has hip-flicked, his body pulling his head
up out of the water. Note that the paddle is kept low.

Fig 72   Guiding the blade (RH). You will quickly learn to do without the
instructor holding the paddle, but may have difficulty keeping it
alongside the boat as you capsize. In this case just the blade can be
held.

SCREW ROLL *(Figs 70 to 72)*

This is a forward roll and does not require moving the hands from the normal grip. There is much less leverage than with the Pawlata and correspondingly better paddle technique and hip-flick are essential.

Technique

1. With the exception that the hands are placed normally, the paddle position and its movement are principally the same as the Pawlata.
2. Leaning well forward is absolutely essential.

3. In the learning stages you may find it helj to slide both hands (equally) towards the no control blade. This will give extra leverag whilst retaining the normal paddle grip.

REVERSE SCREW ROL
(Fig 73)

Being a reverse roll, it starts with the canoei leaning backwards and the paddle towarc the stern of the boat. A combined sitting u and forward sculling action is responsible f righting the boat. The advantage of a revers roll is that if you capsize in moving water yc are likely to be forced into a leaning bacl wards position.

Fig 73   *Reverse screw roll (RH). This roll has an uncomfortable wind-up, unfair when compared with the ease with which the roll itself can be performed. Note how contorted Nicholas's right arm becomes as he takes up the starting position. It is quite common to capsize as you are getting ready.*

echnique

From a normal paddle position, lift your
ntrol hand to the opposite side of your
ad.

Lean backwards (if necessary until your
ad rests on the rear deck) and wind up your
ntrol wrist by flexing it backwards.

Capsize and reach for the control blade to
eak the surface on its own side of the
at. Your wrist should still be flexed.

To roll, simply sit up, hip-flick and scull.

FLOAT AND HAND ROLLS *(Fig 74)*

These are rolls without a paddle, using any
object such as a piece of wood (or swimming
float) in one hand, or nothing at all. Neither roll
is of much use on open water, but both are
used to develop hip-flicks and general co-
ordination. There are many different techniques, although they fall into two groups:

1. Using your float or hand like the blade of a
paddle in a conventional roll and your arm
acting as the shaft. The 'blade' sculls as you
hip-flick.

*74   Hand rolling. The ultimate in co-ordination of body movement is rolling
with no paddle. There are no tricks, although a few tips will help. Peter
is giving a splendid demonstration of the top hand being thrown over
the boat during the hip-flick, to act like a counterbalance weight.*

2. As above, but using the float or your hand as the blade in a hanging support stroke, one downward thrust of the 'blade' and a hip-flick and you are up.

Whichever method you adopt, it is essential to lower your centre of gravity immediately after the hip-flick. This is done by leaning quickly forwards or backwards. It will add power to your hip action if you throw your non working arm over the boat like a counterbalance weight.

ROLLING PRACTICE

Rolling needs constant practice. It may not b needed often in a real situation, but when it you have to get it right. Practise rolling on bo sides, in clean and in murky water, wearir minimum and wearing maximum clothin and in warm and in cold weather.

0 Rescues

contrast to Eskimo rolling, which is about
scuing yourself, the techniques that follow
plain how another paddler can help you.
u may be still in your boat (upsidedown) or
eady out of it. (All the explanations are
itten as if you are the person who needs to
rescued.)

ESKIMO RESCUE
(Figs 75 to 77)

You will have realised from the introduction to
the rolling chapter, that if an Eskimo were to
capsize and could not roll, he would have the
greatest difficulty in getting out.

75 *Waiting for rescue. It is important to keep the hands away from the
boat in the cowboy's 'hands-up' position. It is then easier for the
rescuer to make contact with you. Note the paddle being kept
alongside the boat by the arm.*

Fig 76 Eskimo bow rescue. The bow of the rescuing boat has made contact
with Nic's hand, and he is using it for support during a hip-flick. If at all
possible, the paddle should be retained throughout.

Somebody, therefore, would have had to help him. In the technique that was developed, the victim had to have enough breath and confidence to stay upsidedown for a while, as well as have a helpful paddler nearby. The modern spraydecks come off easily and there is no problem getting out of the boat. To be able to stay in it, however, means that there are none of the problems of waterlogged boat and getting you back in. All you need to do is be able to hold your breath for a moment and attract the attention of a competent paddler nearby.

Technique

1. After capsizing, keep a tight grip with your knees, put your arms out of the water, one on each side of the boat, and bang a few times loudly and slowly. This is to attract attention. (You should let your paddle float alongside the boat, keeping it in place with an arm.)

2. Turn your hands to a cowboy's 'hands-up' position, a little way from the sides of the boat and move them slowly forwards and backwards from bow to stern.

You can now be rescued by one of two techniques:

Bow Approach

1. The alerted rescuer paddles towards you so that the bow of his boat makes contact with one of your hands. He must approach quickly and under control. Not being able to stop in time could damage your hand or boat.

2. Once you have hold of the rescuer's bow it is a simple matter for you to hip-flick up.

3. The rescuer will need to paddle very gently into your hands, otherwise his boat can be pushed away by your hip-flicking action.

77 *Eskimo paddle rescue. Carol has put her boat alongside the upturned one, laid her paddles across the gap between them and directed Nic's hand onto the shaft. He is adjusting his grip ready to hip-flick, during which Carol will try to ease the pressure of the paddle on the upturned boat, pressure which might otherwise keep it upsidedown.*

addle Approach

his is safer than the bow approach, as there
less risk of the rescuer damaging your hand
boat, and he can also help you up if you are
ed or injured.

The alerted rescuer must position himself
ongside your capsized boat. He may do this
paddling in sideways with a draw stroke, by
proaching forwards from either end, or by
ddling in straight for the side of your boat
d turning at the last moment with a reverse
eep stroke. The latter option is the fastest
d most controlled.

When alongside, the rescuer places his
ddle across the two boats, takes hold of
ur hand nearest to him and places it on the
ddle shaft.

You can now flick up, whilst the rescuer

lifts the shaft slightly to reduce pressure on the
upturned hull.

4. It is very important for you to wait for the
rescuer to guide your hand nearest to him,
and important that the rescuer does so. To
grab the blade that may be visible on the
non-rescuing side of you, and try to hip-flick
up on it, is extremely difficult and will usually
result in you coming out of your boat.

PADDLES IN RESCUES

The rescues that follow are for use when you
are out of your boat. A possible problem is for
you to keep hold of your paddle and for the
rescuer to have his hands free of paddles in
order to rescue you. If you accidentally let
yours go, leave it and retrieve it later. The

Fig 78 X-rescue. The rescuer can empty Amelia's boat by rocking it across his deck, whilst she stays in sight and looks after the paddles. Nic is very stable, as the boat across his deck acts like an outrigger as he leans from one side to the other.

rescuer may need to use his in the rescue, keep it across his lap or pass it to you to look after.

X-RESCUE *(Figs 78 & 79)*

This can be performed by a single canoeist and is best suited to fairly calm conditions.

Technique

The idea is for the rescuer to empty your boat by rocking it across his own deck and then helping you back in.

1. The rescuer paddles up to you, takes hold of the end of your boat and tells you to go to the front of his own and hold on. Sending you to the end of his boat enables him to keep an eye on you. It has been known for someone

being rescued to drift off while his boat wa[s] being emptied.

2. The rescuer leaves your boat upsidedov[n] and with a jerking action, lifts one end ar[d] pulls the boat across his front deck. The re[s] cuer will find this easier if he lifts the bow. (Th[e] design of the cockpit normally means that th[e] boat will scoop up less water if lifted bow firs[t])

3. With your boat across his, the rescu[er] should be able to rock it from side to side [to] empty out the water. He can lean as much [as] he likes, as your boat acts like an outrigg[er] and makes it almost impossible for him [to] capsize.

4. When your boat is empty, the rescu[er] turns it the right way up and puts it on th[e] water alongside his but the opposite w[ay] round.

5. You are instructed to work your way alo[ng] between the two boats. The rescuer res[ts] across the front deck of your boat in order

79 Re-entry after rescue. After emptying her boat, Nic needs to get Amelia
    back in it. He has brought her boat alongside his, but the other way
    round, and braced steady with his weight on the paddles. Few people
    – particularly youngsters – have enough strength to simply climb back
    in, and it is necessary to stay in the water and slide your feet and legs in
    first. Your body then follows.

bilise it, in preparation for re-entry.

You should lay on your back, feet towards
cockpit, place one hand on the rescuer's
ck and the other on the back of your cock-
. Leave your body in the water and put your
t into the boat. Do not try and lift your body
ar of the water and into the boat. You will be
tired or not strong enough anyway!

You are now able to wriggle your legs back
o the boat and your body will follow. All the
e, the rescuer has been steadying the exer-
e by lying across your deck and holding
ht.

The rescuer helps you with your spraydeck
d checks that his own was not loosened
ring the rescue.

If you are suitably confident and experi-
ced you may be able to assist with the
cue. This may be by helping to get the
capsized boat across the rescuer's deck, or
by helping with the rocking/emptying action.

RAFTED X-RESCUE
(Figs 80 & 81)

This requires two rescuers and is used in
rougher water or where a more stable rescue
is necessary. It is possible to empty a completely waterlogged boat and no help from
you is required.

Technique

1. This is almost exactly the same as the
basic X-rescue, except that a second rescuer
is rafted alongside the first and stabilises him.
2. If your boat has a lot of water in it, making it

Fig 80   Rafted X-Rescue. Two rescuing boats rafted together form a very
         stable platform for the emptying routine. In addition, the combined
         strengths of Charlie and Nicholas make it easier to pull the upturned
         boats across their decks, and the extra hands can look after all the
         paddles. The positioning of boats in this rescue would be ideal for
         repairing a holed hull. If this had been the case, however, Dominic
         would have climbed out of his damaged boat onto the back of the raft,
         thus avoiding getting unnecessarily wet (and probably cold).

too heavy to lift across the deck without risk of
damage, an alternative emptying technique is
used. One of the rescuers places your boat
alongside his own, turns the cockpit towards
him, holds the top edge of it and eases it up
sideways. In this way it is possible to drain
nearly all the water out without bearing any
real weight. The second rescuer will need to
stabilise his colleague securely.

HI-RESCUE *(Fig 82)*

This is for use in similar circumstances to th
rafted-X, although it is probably more stab
and easier for you to re-enter. It requires tw
rescuers.

81   Rescuing a waterlogged boat. This requires a stable rescue technique,
in this case the rafted-X. Scott is lying (hidden) across the back of
Andrew's boat to stabilise it, while the latter lifts the flooded boat
sideways and allows the water to pour out of the cockpit. (The principle
is the same as shown in Fig 36). Rescuers require spraydecks in all the
techniques, a need that is particularly obvious in this instance.

echnique

The basic principle of your position during
e rescue is as outlined for other rescues.

Your boat is manoeuvred between the two
scuers, who brace all three boats together
¬ putting all available paddles across their
ps.

One end of your boat (preferably the bow)
lifted onto the bridge made by the paddle
afts, taking care not to damage them.

4. The boat is rocked across this bridge.
5. You can help with the rocking, as one end
of your boat is moving up and down just above
your head. This is particularly helpful if the boat
has a lot of water in it.
6. The empty boat is turned the right way up
and lodged between the two rescuers.
7. You can re-enter as in the X-rescue or by
clambering across the three-boat raft.

*Fig 82   HI-Rescue. The rescuers have used all the paddles to make a bridge
between their boats and can rock the capsized boat across it. Dominic
has the end of his upturned boat waivering above his head and can
help with the rocking action. Not only must he keep hold of the rescuer
in the interests of safety, but it is only by doing so that he has the
leverage to help rock his own boat. You will notice that the paddle
blades lie flat across Nicholas' lap, while the upright blades on
Charlie's side extend beyond the edge of his boat. This reduces the
possibility of any damage to either paddles or spraydecks.*

1 Moving Water Techniques

hen water moves, it follows the line of least sistance, and if a rock is in the way, the ater will flow round it. You and your boat, wever, are not fixed like rocks and moving ater will normally sweep you along with it. it if you offer some resistance by paddling, e water gives in and flows round you, leaving u to move about. How well you can move out will depend on your technique, the rength of the current and whether you are sitioned across it or in line with it.

IVER CONDITIONS

vers are natural watercourses that drain the ater from mountains and pastures and allow to run into lakes or the sea. In a perfect tuation, the water would all run straight ownhill (the line of least resistance), but there e bends, narrows, ledges and other ob-ructions on the way.

rag

here water comes into contact with the river ank or bed, there is some resistance against e mud or gravel or rock from which it is ade. This slows the water down over the eas of contact and is called *drag*. Thus a ver flows fastest in the middle (away from the rag of the banks) and where it is deepest (the urface being away from the drag of the river ed).

Rapid (Fig 83)

This is created where there is a restriction in the amount of space through which the river can flow and the water is forced to speed up. It occurs where the river narrows (as in a gorge or canyon) or where it suddenly becomes shallower. Both situations are characterised by a series of standing waves (so called because they are stationary) across the river, starting at a point just downstream of the start of the obstruction. Rapids are good fun as long as you maintain enough water speed to be able to steer.

Eddy (Fig 83)

This is the swirling effect created at the back of an obstruction by the water being forced to go round it. The same effect is also created when water flows past a small inlet in the river bank.

The water in an eddy may be slack or be moving in the opposite direction to the main stream. It is of great value to the canoeist as a stopping place.

Waterfall

A rock fault that creates a sudden drop in the river-bed creates a waterfall. A canoe is often able to negotiate the small ones, although the shallow water on the edge of the fall may damage the boat.

Weir

This is really a man-made waterfall and is usually constructed so that the flow of water can be regulated by sluice gates. There are often steel posts and concrete ledges hidden beneath the surface and these can cause serious injuries, particularly in a capsize. Do not venture near weirs without a suitably experienced and qualified instructor.

Stopper Wave *(Fig 84)*

When water falls (waterfall or weir) and hits the river bed, it is forced up again by the water coming behind it and often curls back into the fall. The point where the two forces of water come towards each other has a holding effect on anything caught in it. Hence it is known as a *stopper wave* and you will need a straight course and plenty of water speed to paddle through it.

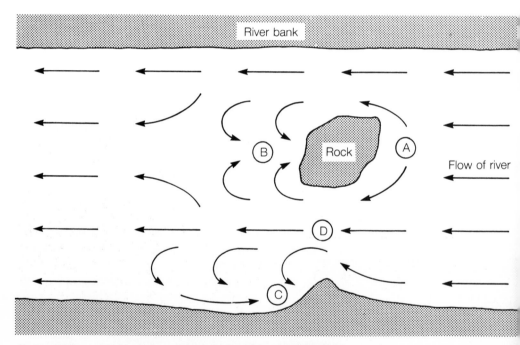

Fig 83   Eddies and rapids. As the water hits the upstream side of the rock, it heaps up before flowing quickly around it – 'A'. This 'heap' of water looks very smooth when you are paddling towards it and should be avoided, as it could pin you dangerously against the rock. As the water rushes past the rock, it creates a sort of vacuum behind it. This is filled by water being pulled in from around, creating a movement of water in the reverse direction to the main flow of the river – 'B'. This is an eddy. A similar situation occurs where the current flows quickly along the river bank and past a bay – 'C'. Where the width of the river has been narrowed by a rock or other obstruction, the water will have to speed up to get through and a rapid is created – 'D'.

If you are unlucky enough to end up sideways in a stopper slot, you are likely to be held
only by it. Escape requires advanced
canoeing ability or immediate assistance from
somebody else. Stopper waves should be
avoided if you do not have suitably experienced people with you, who are able to
advise, supervise and rescue if necessary.

RIVER TECHNIQUES

Lean

If you are paddling against the stream (upstream) or with it (downstream) keep the boat
level. As soon as you position the boat across
the stream, it is necessary to lean downstream and allow the moving water to flow

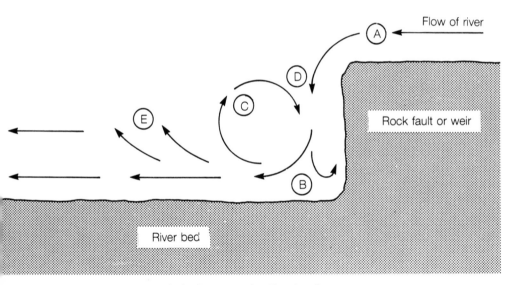

Flow of river

A

D

C

E

Rock fault or weir

B

River bed

Fig 84 Stoppers and standing waves. As the river approaches the edge of a
fall, it usually becomes shallow and speeds up – 'A'. It falls to the river
bed, some curling back towards the fall, but most continuing on – 'B'.
It cannot, however, continue on uninterrupted, as the slower moving
water already below the fall stops it. It is therefore forced up – 'C'. A
slight vacuum will have been caused by the falling water, and the rising
water will move to fill it – 'D'. This is the stopper wave. There are now
two forces of water meeting and they have a holding effect on anything
caught in the slot between them. Not all the water goes into the
stopper wave, some coming forceably to the surface further
downstream and creating standing waves – 'E'. These are so called as
they have no ground speed.

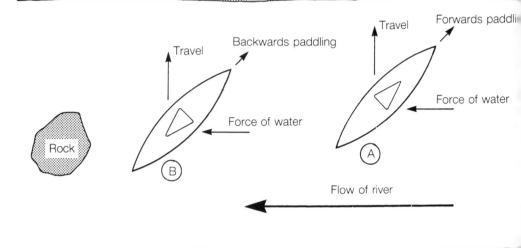

Fig 85   Ferry-gliding. Boat 'A' is moving across the river by being pointed
        upstream, angled slightly towards the required direction of travel and
        paddled forwards. Boat 'B' has been travelling downstream and must
        avoid the rock. It is immediately paddled backwards, and angled
        slightly towards the required direction of travel. In all instances, the
        angle of the boat to the water will depend on the speed of the water
        and the power of the paddling.

under your boat. Even a momentary lean upstream will give the oncoming water an opportunity to put pressure on the deck and capsize
you instantaneously.

Bear in mind that in a strong eddy the water
is flowing in the opposite direction to the main
stream, necessitating a lean in the opposite
direction.

Ferry-glide *(Fig 85)*

If you want to cross a river and you point your
boat to the other side and paddle, you will drift
downstream and not arrive at your destina-
tion. Watch a duck and you will see that it
angles itself to the stream depending on the
speed of the water. You will need to do the
same, the direction of the moving water com-

bining with the direction of your paddling
move you in a different direction altogether.
is called *ferry-gliding* and is derived from th
action of the many river ferry boats that hav
to adopt a similar technique.

Technique

1. Position yourself alongside the bank facir
upstream.
2. Angle the front of the boat out a little an
paddle forwards.
3. Fix the point on the opposite bank when
you want to finish, and use trial and error
your boat angle and paddling power until yc
get there.
4. Remember to lean downstream and (part
cularly in faster flowing water) you may need t

ddle on the downstream side only. If you
ddle on the upstream side, you run the risk
he oncoming water pushing your upstream
de under the boat.

You will soon get a feel for the angle at
ich to steer, as well as confidence in lean-
the boat. Practise backwards as well, i.e.
erse ferry gliding.

se

s used not only to travel across moving
ter, but also to avoid dangerous obstacles.
ou are paddling downstream and see a
ck directly in front of you, your instinct will be
aim to one side and paddle fast. As you
gle your boat, however, the flow of the river
hit your upstream side and wash you even
ter downstream, directly onto the rock.
s is dangerous, as it will force you into an
stream lean and instant capsize. The force
water may be sufficient to break the boat in
f, possibly trapping your legs at the same
e. A similar situation can occur with over-
nging trees.

The answer is to reverse ferry-glide, by
ddling backwards and angling the back
ern) of your boat in the direction you want to
. A few powerful strokes will position you far
ough to one side of the obstacle to be able
paddle on again forwards in safety.

reak Out *(Fig 86)*

is is the technique for getting out of the main
ream into an eddy. You may want to inspect
rapid, see that others go past safely or
nply get out and have a rest.

echnique

Look for the eddy. It may be behind a rock
in an inlet.

Maintain water speed and position yourself
so that your bow will go into the eddy immediately downstream of the obstruction that
causes it.

3. Your last stroke to turn the bow into the
eddy should be a powerful forward sweep
stroke.

4. With the bow in, stop paddling. The bow
will be stopped by the eddy, but your stern will
be swept on by the main flow of the river.

5. Help the turn by doing a reverse sweep (on
the inside of the turn) flattened out a little to
give support. This stroke can be turned into a
bow draw (to get the bow tight into the eddy)
and then into a forward paddling stroke to
stop any continuing downstream movement.

6. Be careful how you lean. The temptation is
to lean into the turn, but if you do so too early
you will still be in the main stream of the river
and be leaning upstream!

7. If your boat position and lean are perfect,
you can break out without a single paddling
stroke.

8. Try it backwards.

Break In

This is for getting out of an eddy into the main
stream.

Technique

1. Drop back a little in the eddy if possible, i.e.
away from the obstruction.

2. Paddle back up the eddy towards the
obstruction.

3. When appropriate, do a forward sweep
stroke to start the turn, and as your bow
enters the main stream, it will be swept downstream. Your stern, however, will be held by
the slack water of the eddy, causing you to
turn sharply.

4. As you turn, lean downstream and do a
reverse sweep (with support) on the inside of
the turn.

5. This reverse sweep can be turned into a bow draw to bring the boat into line with the flow of the river, and then into a forward paddling stroke to give you water speed.

6. A break-in should also be practised without using your paddle, as well as backwards.

Mooring

If you are alongside the bank, either alone or as part of a raft, always face upstream. Only in this way can you see anything being swept towards you.

Safety on Rapids

The rule of 'less than three there should ne' be' is particularly important. Moving water c quickly catch you unawares and jam y against a rock or capsize you. The immedia assistance of others is vital. Always lo closely at unfamiliar stretches before go' afloat, be sure to wear a crash hat and a w fitting buoyancy aid, and check that your bo is intact and has a footrest and plenty buoyancy.

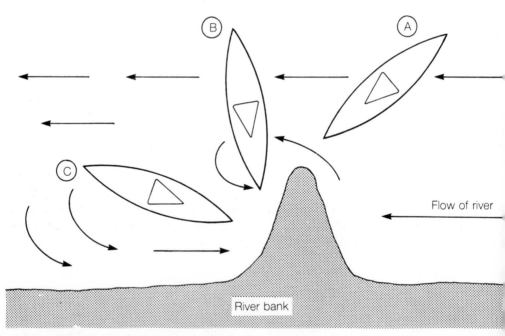

Fig 86 *Breaking out. A canoeist travelling downstream should spot the break-out opportunity and angle his bow to tuck in tight behind the obstruction – 'A'. When the bow is in the shelter of the obstruction, it is in an eddy, where the water is stationary or moving in the opposite direction to the river. This holds the bow still, whilst the stern is swept on by the main flow – 'B'. By leaning and using strokes as described in the text, the boat will complete the turn and end up in the sheltered waters of the eddy – 'C'.*

he techniques of breaking-in, breaking-
and ferry-gliding are essential for all this
rk, although as your skill develops, you may
different strokes to achieve the same
ults. The more advanced water conditions
ystacks, boils, whirlpools) and techniques
gh-crossing, looping) are beyond the scope
his book.

IVER GRADING

system has been devised whereby rivers
be classified according to level of diffi-
ty. There are six grades:

ade I Not difficult: regular stream, waves,
ids and simple obstructions.

ade II Moderately Difficult: irregular stream
d waves. Medium rapids and small stop-
rs, eddies and drops. Route easy to find.

ade III Difficult: larger waves and rapids,
quent drops and obstructions with associ-
d conditions. Route still recognisable.

ade IV Very Difficult: as Grade III but with
ger rapids, obstructions and associated
nditions. Route not easy to recognise.

ade V Extremely Difficult: conditions al-
ys require prior inspection.

ade VI Limit of Practicability: cannot be
ddled without serious risk to life.

SEA CONDITIONS

Although the sea is kept topped-up by fresh
water from the rivers and rain, it retains its
saltiness and exhibits conditions fun-
damentally different from rivers.

Waves

Most waves at sea are caused by the wind,
and the stronger the wind and the longer the
distance it has been able to blow across the
water, the bigger the waves. All these waves
move, i.e. they are not standing waves.

Tide

This is the movement of water up and down
the beach and is caused by the positions of
the moon and the sun and their corresponding gravitational pulls on the earth.

Tidal Stream

This is the movement of water along the coast
and is similar to the flow of a river. Unlike a
river, it changes direction in time with the
change of the tide. Tidal streams can attain
speeds as fast as a river.

Tidal Race

This is where the sea is forced through a
narrow gap and is similar to a river rapid. It is
most frequent between the mainland and an
off-shore island. The water can reach enor-
mous speeds (up to 18 kph) and the great
scale of the sea can make a race a very
frightening situation. It changes direction with
the tide.

Fig 87   Skeg. Racing and touring boats are able to hold a straight course by having a long waterline, i.e. the hull keeps its shape in the water for the entire length of the boat. Slalom and general purpose boats are designed to be more manoeuvrable. A device can be made, that slides onto the back of the boat and acts like a fixed rudder. It is called a skeg and is held in place by tying it to a deckline or the back of the cockpit. Surf kayaks and skis may have built-in skegs.

Fig 88   Bracing. Nicholas is being swept in sideways by a breaking wave and is keeping his balance by holding a bracing stroke in the upsurge of water inside the wave. He is paddling a surf-ski.

verfall

is is also like a river rapid, but created when e sea has to pass through a shallower area. is may be a sandbank or rocky ledge, and it quite common for conditions to be such that race and an overfall occur together. This ombination, together with a strong and unvourable wind, can create horrific water nditions, beyond many motorised boats d completely out of the question for kayaks.

urf

his is where a wave builds up and then eaks as a result of the water getting too allow to support the wave's height. Surf is eated above off-shore sandbanks, but is ost common on beaches. The best are ently sloping sandy beaches, particularly ose which face the prevailing wind (southest to west) and where the wind has been le to travel a long way without interruption. nce the wave has broken, it produces foamy ater called *soup*.

EA TECHNIQUES

ne scope of this book covers little more an canoeing in sheltered bays or small surf, way from many of the conditions so far described.

teering *(Fig 87)*

Vind and waves will cause the general purose boat to change course frequently. Good se of sweep strokes can correct this, but a oat with a longer waterline or one equipped vith a skeg is preferable.

Lean

Ordinary sea waves move in relation to the ground beneath them. If it is necessary to lean (perhaps being swept sideways in surf), always lean into the wave (upstream). If you lean towards the beach, i.e. downstream, the wave will sweep you along and force your gunwale to cut into the water and capsize you. The lean at sea is, therefore, in completely the opposite direction to the lean on a river.

Stern Rudder

If a wave comes up behind you and threatens to turn you sideways, a stern rudder will steer you back on course. It is a very important stroke in surf.

Brace *(Fig 88)*

If you find yourself swept sideways by a wave, lean into it and brace yourself by sticking the blade into the wave. Surf is one of the few situations where this stroke is not only possible, but also essential and often very effective (*see* 'Bracing Strokes').

Safety in Surf

Waves can move deceptively quickly and one can pick you up suddenly and shoot you forward like a rocket. In any surf situation, take great care to keep away from other canoeists (only one on any one wave) and do not surf amongst swimmers. If you are on course for a collision of any sort and cannot find the strength or technique to avoid it, capsize. The action of your body burying itself into the wave will have a sudden braking effect and should prevent the accident.

12   Where to Learn

The national organisation for all sports is the Sports Council. Each separate sport has its own national body, e.g. Amateur Athletics Association, all of which are affiliated to the Sports Council.

British Canoe Union

The BCU is the national body representing all aspects of canoeing and kayaking within the UK. It is a member of the International Canoe Federation, which is affiliated to the International Olympic Committee. Within the BCU are separate associations representing Scotland, Wales and Northern Ireland, and the whole area is divided into administrative regions. Each region has a Regional Coaching Organiser, who shares his work amongst a number of Local Coaching Organisers. The BCU has an excellent Coaching Scheme, which trains and examines instructors and coaches at every level and in every branch of the sport. Newcomers to the sport normally work their way up through one of the sets of graded tests. There are the Proficiency Tests, which require paddling and touring skills and are ideally suited for those wanting to go on day trips or canoe camping expeditions: the Star Tests, which examine paddling skills and background knowledge only; and the Placid Water Tests and Awards, which relate to the skills of using flat water racing boats.

These series of tests cover every aspect of the sport, be it inland or at sea, in competition or general purpose boats of a kayak or Canadian canoe design and on flat or moving water. Youngsters having achieved the highest grade in any series will have reached a very proficient paddling standard. You can be come an individual member of the BCU an take advantage of its many services and fac ties.

Canoe Clubs

These are not only where you can be taugh but also where you will find many friends wi whom to paddle. There will also be opportur ties to try some or all of the competitive ar recreational branches of the sport, and yo knowledge from this book will be an excelle basis for whichever activity your interest take you into. A club will usually have its ow headquarters and boathouse, as well as fac ties for fitness training and social activitie Members often have the opportunity to mal their own boats, and there is normally a hea thy trade in secondhand equipment.

A very specialist type of club is the Corps Canoe Lifeguards, which exists to provide service to the community, by patrollin beaches or other potentially dangerou waters used by the public. The corps has i own series of appropriate life-saving tests an awards.

Youth Organisations

Many have adopted canoeing as part of multi-activity programme, ranging from once-a-year water weekend to a regula meeting of a special canoeing group. Mar youth organisations have their own awar schemes, although these normally requir one of the BCU tests or awards as a pre requisite. Canoeing may also be part of

Fig 89   Messing about in boats. This is always fun, and there are all sorts of
games in canoes and kayaks that do not fall under any of the sporting
headings. In this instance, Lisa's bow has been lifted so that her boat
dives backwards, while Amelia looks on from an already sinking boat.
These pranks are possible, partly because of the low volume of
modern boats and partly by having some water in them. Safety
precautions are critical and the boats must be strong enough to
withstand the additional strain.

Duke of Edinburgh Award Scheme program-me. A very large number of young people are first introduced to the sport during the course of youth club activity.

Activity Centres

These may be run by the Sports Council, a Local Council, an Education Authority or privately. They employ full-time staff, provide equipment of a high standard and normally offer facilities such as changing rooms, showers, catering and residential accommodation. The centres usually run a wide range of canoeing courses (either on a purely leisure basis or geared to a BCU award) on a one-day, full weekend or all week basis. Canoeing will seldom be the only sport represented, sailing and other water-sports being regular alternatives. Other activities will depend on location, and may include pony-trekking, climbing, fishing, surfing, pot-holing, and fell-walking.

There is a lot to learn about canoeing and lots of places to learn it. Addresses of local instructors and clubs, together with details of tests, awards and courses are all available from the BCU. Its address is: British Canoe Union, Flexel House, 45/47 High Street, Addlestone, Surrey KT15 1JV.

13 Where to Paddle

Water is all you need, but are you allowed to use it? This is a question that a canoeist does not always think to ask, but water is as much somebody's property as is a house or a garden. The British Isles is a little unusual in this respect, the waters of many other countries being the property of the State and free for all to use.

Using water without permission is trespass, and the law in this respect is not the same for Scotland and Northern Ireland as it is for England and Wales. In addition, the general situation for rivers is not the same for the sea.

THE RIVERS

Ownership

The owner of a river may not be the person who owns the banks, and (as rivers are often county boundaries) each bank and each half of the river may be in different hands. Furthermore, the fishing rights may have been sold to yet another person. The control of some rivers has passed into the hands of water authorities, e.g. Thames Conservancy.

Objections

An objection to you paddling a river may purely be that the owner(s) wants the water to himself. Normally, however, the objection is made because some believe that boats disturb the breeding and catching of fish. Individuals often pay large sums for the right to fish a river and the owners might lose this

source of income if the river were to become a general boating area. Some forms of angling have a particular season and canoeing may be allowed outside these seasons.

Right of Navigation

Certain rivers have been used by boats for such a long time that they have been classified as *ancient navigations* and any craft is free to travel along them, for example the lower part of the River Wye. In some cases they can only be used after payment of a fee, such as the River Thames. Of the remaining rivers, the law states that a right of navigation only exists if there has been uninterrupted and unchallenged use over a long period of time. This is very difficult to prove and the permission of the owner(s) is normally required.

Permission

For each canoeist to find the river owner(s) and ask his permission would be impractical. The BCU, therefore, has appointed a National Access Officer, whose task it is to liaise with river owners, landowners, anglers and water authorities for the use of their water. He also administers the River Advisory Scheme whereby suitably experienced and knowledgeable local people are elected as advisors for particular areas. Every canoeist should seek advice about unfamiliar waters from the appropriate River Advisor. His address is available from the BCU, as are guides to all the rivers in the UK.

akes

ne situation is essentially the same as for vers, although use of lakes attracts fewer bjections from fishermen. Some, such as the orfolk Broads, are ancient navigations, ome have been converted by Local Councils to boating lakes and some still require dvice from the River Advisor. Bear in mind at although lakes do not flow like rivers, they an present rough and exposed conditions ot unlike the sea.

Canals

The main network is the property of British Waterways and a licence is required from them. Reduced rates are available to BCU members. The placid waters of canals are ideal for touring and can take you deep into peaceful countryside.

90   Pool canoeing. Not only do swimming pools provide ideal conditions for learning skills such as eskimo rolling, but they are invaluable in introducing the disabled to the fun of the water and the challenge of the sport. Anna is building up her strength and technique slowly and comfortably before venturing out onto open water.

THE SEA

In general terms, the sea is owned by the Crown and is free for all to use. Not so the beaches, however, which can be privately owned or otherwise protected. It may be possible, therefore, to paddle a stretch of coast, but not be allowed to go near the shore or land on it.

Local Councils

By-laws are sometimes passed for certain beaches, in order to restrict swimming to safer areas or to keep canoeists and other boats away from swimmers. The restrictions for swimmers and for canoeists and surfers are marked by flags of special colours, and any regulations should be strictly adhered to.

Harbour Authorities

It is inadvisable for a canoe to go near any motorised vessels or the harbours and commercial docks which they use. Some harbour authorities have the backing of a by-law to prevent your entry or to regulate it by displaying coded symbols. If you must enter and are allowed to, a fee may be demanded.

Marine Reserves

These have been established to protect stretches of the coastline and/or adjacent waters used by important sea-birds and oth[er] marine life. Access may be totally restricte[d] or restricted during breeding seasons.

H.M. Forces

Certain areas are set aside for military exe[r]cises and passage through them is eith[er] forbidden altogether or regulated by flag si[g]nals. The areas are clearly marked on admir[al]ty charts.

Permission

The Sea Touring Committee of the BCU h[as] appointed a number of Coastal Advisors, or [a] similar basis to the River Advisory Service. T[he] appropriate one will be able to give you all t[he] information you need for your chosen are[a.]

SWIMMING POOLS

It is easy to forget these, but they provide ide[al] training areas. Permission is obviously r[e]quired from the Local Council or School and [is] likely to be restricted to canoe clubs. You w[ill] be required to clean your boats before they g[o] into the pool, possibly with a disinfectant.

4 Other Disciplines

ost of the book has been about general ayaking techniques and will have provided bu with an excellent foundation for taking art in a variety of other *disciplines*. These are e specialised forms of the sport, most of hich are of a competitive nature. Each of the sciplines is administered by a specialist ommittee of the British Canoe Union and publishes an annual handbook detailing the current rules, events and active paddlers. It is necessary to be a member of the BCU (or one of its national associations) in order to compete in official competitions, which may be of a local, regional, national or international nature. At the time of writing, only sprint racing is an Olympic event. Slalom was included in 1972,

g 91   *Sprint kayak. These are lightweight craft for increased speed, but have reduced rigidity as a consequence. They need to be handled carefully, particularly when being emptied. Note the increased length, decreased width and different overall shape compared with the general purpose boats. The noticeably large cockpit makes getting in and out easier, and is possible as sprint paddlers do not need to jam their knees up under the deck.*

but has not appeared since due to the difficulties in finding or building a suitable course.

SPRINT RACING

This takes place on courses that are specially designed to be as flat and as calm as possible. Distances of between 500 metres and 10,000 metres are paddled, but as an actual course is rarely 10,000 metres in length, turns may be required at one or both ends. The events are for single, double or four seater kayaks (known as K1, K2 and K4 respectively) and single or double seater canoes (C1 and C2). In a sprint kayak *(Fig 91)*, the paddler keeps his knees together in the centre of the large cockpit, but may wear a spraydeck, both for warmth and as a protection from drips off the paddle. The sprint canoe has almost no deck and the paddler kneels on one knee.

The object of a race is to cover the distance in the fastest time possible. For this, the boats need to be long and narrow, in order to increase speed and directional stability. However, regulations stipulate a maximum length and a minimum width and weight for each of the different types. Competitors require strength, stamina and a technique which enables them to perform an identical paddling movement repeatedly. In order not to break this stroke rhythm, steering is achieved by a special foot-controlled rudder. For those starting sprint racing, there is a graded series of tests and awards, related to both skill and timed distance achievements. Junior, ladies and men compete over a different range of distances, but they all start in the lowest division. At the end of a season, paddlers may be promoted to a higher one, depending on results. Sprint racing is increasing in popularity but needs to be pursued in a club environment. Major events are held on the purpose-built course at Holme Pierrepont in Notting-

ham, which also has all the facilities require for International competition.

MARATHON RACING

This is similar to sprint racing, but can tak place on any open water – inland or at sea and over almost any distance. The longe marathon race in the UK is from Devizes Westminster, being 125 miles in length ar involving 72 portages. A portage is where th boat has to be carried around an obstac such as a weir or lock. Marathon is open any style of boat, as long as it is within th length and width limits set for sprint racin There are nine divisions, enabling races to b staged for every level of ability. It is very easy organise a race, particularly at club level, ar the freedom of choice of water and boat making it a very popular branch of the spor

SLALOM *(Fig 92)*

This is perhaps the most well-known of th competitive disciplines, possibly because the exciting nature of the water on which takes place. The course is a series of gate each being two poles suspended above a eddy, standing wave or other interesting are of a rapid or weir stream. The gates are num bered, as well as marked to indicate wheth to go through forwards or backwards. The must be negotiated in numeric sequence leaving the red and white striped poles on th left, and the green and white ones on the righ Penalty points are awarded for touching, mis sing out or going the wrong way through gate, and these are added to the time taken t complete the course. Kayaks are all sing seater (K1), but canoes compete as sing (C1) or double (C2). The high degree of man oeuvrability required means that boats mus ave a short waterline, but there is a minimum ermitted length, as well as width. They are so made as low as possible (minimum buoyancy), in order that the bow or stern can e dipped under a pole when entering or aving a gate.

Strict safety regulations apply to equipment nd the organisation of events, and rescuers ill often be positioned on the bank adjacent the more difficult stretches of the course. A visional system operates and promotion ay occur immediately following a good re- llt or at the end of a season. British paddlers o very well at World Championship events, everal of them having won gold medals.

WILD WATER RACING

This must take place on a mountain river, over a distance of at least three kilometres and with stretches of at least Grade III water. Two skills are needed, the ability to keep up a regular power stroke, and the ability to read the water conditions ahead. The boat requires speed and directional stability and will have a hull design similar to the sprint racing craft, but with increased volume and strength in order to give extra buoyancy and resilience in the rough water. Competing craft may be K1, C1 or C2 and a divisional system operates to segregate the differing performances of men,

ig 92   Slalom. The line through the gate number means that it must be
        negotiated forwards from the other side. A reverse gate would have
        been marked by the letter 'R'. Many youngsters compete in slalom
        competitions as part of their general canoeing activity.

ladies, youths and juniors. Strict safety regulations have to be observed, similar to those of slalom.

SURF *(Fig 93)*

This is the only competitive discipline in which the winner emerges from points being awarded for his skill, rather than for completing a course against the clock. The best surf is usually found on gently sloping sandy beaches that face between west and south. Those of South Wales, and North Devon and Cornwall are well-known. Slalom and general purpose boats perform well, and some of their activity can be very acrobatic.

Craft *(Fig 94)*

Two specialised craft have been developed. The *surf kayak* has all the characteristics of a kayak, but is the shape and size of a surf board. The *surf-ski,* however, is little more than a surfboard on which you sit and paddle. It has recesses for your bottom and heels with straps to hold you on, but easy to release if necessary. Both craft grip the wave well, but the ski tends to be preferred, as it cannot fill up with water – if you capsize, you simply turn it upright again and climb back on.

Judging involves watching a paddler for a period of twenty minutes. Each of his runs on a wave is marked out of ten and the scores for the best five are added together for the overall

Fig 93   Surf gymnastics. This amazing looking stunt is not difficult to produce in surf and is a feature of using slalom kayaks. Gary Adcock, three times British Slalom Paddle Surf Champion, is seen here competing in the 1984 Kerno Championships.

ig 94　Surf-ski. A purpose built boat, being the principles of a kayak
superimposed on a surf board. You can see the recesses and straps
for the feet and Charlie is carrying the ski with his shoulder under the
thigh strap. Note the leash, which is tied to the paddler's ankle in order
to maintain contact after a capsize.

result. The different designs of boat compete in their own events, as do men, ladies and juniors.

In addition to normal safety regulations, there is a strict discipline of only one boat being allowed on a wave at any one time. The sport is currently practiced in relatively few countries.

CANOE POLO *(Fig 95)*

This is a 5-a-side team game, played in miniature kayaks (called BATs) of between two and three metres in length. It is normally played in a large swimming pool and the object is for a plastic football to be thrown to score a goal, by hitting a one metre square board suspende two metres above the water. There is a goal each end, and the ball may be stopped by paddle blade, but not propelled by it. Whoeve is in possession of the ball may be tackled, a action that may include capsizing. The gam is fast and very strenuous.

Players wear crash hats and buoyancy aid to protect themselves against swirling pad dles and accidental ramming. Boats hav rounded ends for safety, and metal tippe paddles are not allowed. Friendly matches ar often played between clubs, and there ar organised regional and national league Other countries sometimes play on ope water, in full size boats and to different rules

Fig 95   Bat polo. The BAT was introduced as the 'baths advanced trainer', but has long since become a basic training boat and the one of choice for canoe polo. The game is seldom played out-of-doors in Britain, although this 'pitch' at Thames Young Mariners must make a welcome change from the heat and stuffiness of a swimming pool.

96 A special kind of freedom. Sea kayaking makes available millions of square miles of water for exploration and adventure. This picture shows Ian Hippach celebrating his crossing of the Arctic Circle, North of Iceland, with a thumbs up. At 14 years of age, he may well be one of the youngest people to have made such a journey. With proper training and proper supervision a lot can be achieved.

CANOE SAILING

Although the origins of canoeing in the UK lie with the sail-assisted Rob Roy boat, this is now the least known of all the disciplines. However, the paddle is no longer used at all and the sailing aspect has been developed to make the craft one of the fastest single-handed dinghies afloat. The sport is often called after the standard size of the sail, being *ten square metres*. Young, old, men and women compete alongside each other, as long as any individual weighs more than 50kg. There is a national training programme and competition takes place at all levels.

SEA TOURING *(Fig 96)*

This is not when somebody takes any boat onto a calm sea and paddles about close to the shore, but when suitably experienced people take specially designed and/or equipped boats onto the sea for a specific purpose. The conditions can become difficult and the skill and experience required can only be built up over a period of time. The reward of the freedom of the sea, however, is well worth the training.

The boat must be long and strong and some of the specially designed ones have many similarities with the original Eskimo

Fig 97 Canoe camping. This takes on a different flavour when using
Canadians. It is possible to prop one up on its paddles and sleep
underneath. The exact method of holding up the canoe depends on its
design, the paddles sometimes resting on the inside of the hull and
sometimes on the thwarts (seats). Three paddles are ideal and should
be fixed, possibly by tying them to the boat and digging the blade
slightly into the ground.

boats. Modern features are incorporated, such as a pump for baling water out of the cockpit area, and bulkheads across the inside of the boat, to make it impossible for water to swamp it entirely. The resulting watertight compartments can be packed with spare clothing, camping gear etc., through hatches in the deck. Other essential equipment includes spare paddles, distress flares, charts and a compass. Sea kayak expeditions have paddled some of the most dangerous seaways in the world, including Cape Horn and the waters of the Arctic North.

CANOE CAMPING (Fig 97

This is not exactly a discipline in its own righ
but a progression from inland and sea touri
that requires certain skills over and abo
normal camping. Apart from all the equipme
needing to be in waterproof containers
compartments, the weight of it must be dist
buted evenly around the canoe. You ca
sometimes benefit from having a heavy bo
or stern according to the direction of the win
but to have one side of the boat heavier tha
the other is a formula for going round in c
cles. The equipment is similar to that of ligh
weight camping and the boat must be packe
in the same order as a rucksack, i.e. what yo
will need first should be packed last. Eve
item must be secured in place and none o

98 *C1 slalom. Martin Hedges is an expert with a single paddle, having been the European Champion in 1980. Here he is demonstrating his mastery of the skills by twisting and using his normally right-handed technique on the left side of the boat.*

99 *J Stroke. David is finishing a forward stroke next to his hips and is twisting the blade for its J action. This is best followed by studying the flexing of his top hand on the T-grip.*

Fig 100   Open Canadian in action. Powering over a small fall just below
           Bickleigh Bridge during the 1983 Exe Descent, Stephen Neal and
           Maurice Histed reap the full benefit from the massive spraydeck that
           can be fitted to these boats.